TABLE OF CONTENTS

FIGURES

ACRONYMS

BBC	British Broadcasting Company
CIA	Central Intelligence Agency
DMZ	Demilitarized Zone
DoD	Department of Defense
DOS	Department of State
DPRK	Democratic People's Republic of Korea
FBI	Federal Bureau of Investigation
IC	Intelligence Community
NPT	Nuclear Non-Proliferation Treaty
ROK	Republic of Korea
SOE	State Owned Enterprise
PMESII	Political, Military, Economic, Social, Infrastructure, Information Systems
UN	United Nations
USSTRATCOM	United States Strategic Command

PREFACE

This report is the product of the United States Strategic Command (USSTRATCOM) J9 STEP internship program. A team of undergraduate and law students from Creighton University worked together to provide this multidisciplinary, unclassified comprehensive report.

The 2011 – 2012 academic team was tasked to identify state – to – state bilateral and multilateral relationship trends between North Korea and China, Japan, Russia, and South Korea.

This project took place September 2011 through May 2012. While the J9 provided the resources and technology for the project, development of the project design, conducting research and analysis, and providing recommendations were left primarily up to the team.

EXECUTIVE SUMMARY

The team was asked to identify current and emerging state-to-state relationship trends North Korea shares with China, Japan, Russia, and South Korea. The team initially analyzed the bilateral relationships in the categories of diplomatic ties, provocations, aid, energy, trade, illicit activity, refugees, and remittances. The relationship strengths were ranked as one of the following: strongly positive, slightly positive, no relationship, slightly negative, strongly negative, and unknown relationship. After evaluating the bilateral relationships, the team used historical examples in conjunction with extensive research to note potential leverage points countries may use to influence North Korea.

INTRODUCTION

The Democratic People's Republic of Korea (DPRK) is headed by the authoritarian Kim Jong-un and his regime of military elites. The state teaches the ideas of diplomatic and economic self-reliance, *Juche*. This *Juche* ideology was meant to show North Korean citizens and the western world that North Korea was independent, not vulnerable to outside influence or Western thought. "The DPRK demonized the US as the ultimate threat to its social system through state-funded propaganda, and molded political, economic, and military policies around the core ideological objective of eventual unification of Korea under Pyongyang's control" (Central Intelligence Agency).

After the Korean War, North Korea (DPRK) was led by President Kim Il-sung. He was succeeded by his son Kim Jong-il in 1980. Under Kim Jong-il's rule, the country experienced years of political and economic mismanagement. As a result, the DPRK now relies heavily on foreign aid, and the population is extremely oppressed. Kim Jong-il's son, Kim Jong-un was named The Great Successor of the DPRK after Kim Jong-il's death in December 2011. Kim Jong-un's official title is The First Secretary which is an alteration from his father's title, Eternal General Secretary. It appears that the Kim regime's political and economic dereliction has continued with Kim Jong-un. Jong-un is furthering North Korea's nuclear program after the country's initial nuclear and missile testing in 2006 and 2009. 2012 marks the centenary of Kim Il-sung's birth and the country declared their focus will be the development of the DPRK economy and improving the quality of life among citizens in order to commemorate the founding father of the country (Central Intelligence Agency).

AREAS OF INTEREST AND METHODOLOGY

The team was allotted eight months to conduct research, provide briefings to USSTRATCOM senior staff, and write a comprehensive report. Research was conducted through a literature review and interviews with academia and experts in both the public and private sectors. The PMESII Model was used to generate a system of methodology. Although PMESII incorporates Political, Military, Economic, Social, Infrastructure, and Information Systems, the team was asked to focus primarily on the Political, Economic, and Social aspects of the model.

The team developed the following thesis statement to determine areas of interest and to structure its research: Gaining a better understanding of North Korea's relationships with China, Japan, Russia, and South Korea will provide alternative opportunities for the United States or allies to achieve mission goals while limiting surprise with regard to North Korean decision-making.

After conducting research through interactions with over 50 subject matter experts, as well as extensive literature reviews from US and international sources, the team determined the following points were of most relevance to the Political, Economic, and Social aspects of North Korea's relationships with China, Japan, Russia, and South Korea: Diplomatic Ties, Provocations, Aid, Energy, Trade, Illicit Activity, Refugees, and Remittances. These aspects of North Korea's relationship were first separated into Political, Economic, and Social categories.

The team determined that Diplomatic Ties and Provocations fell under the Political category; Aid, Energy, and Trade fell under Economic; and, Illicit Activity, Refugees, and Remittances fell under Social. Thus, the team will first discuss each of these aspects (Diplomatic, Provocations, Aid, Energy, Trade, Illicit, Refugees, and Remittances) in order of their category (Political, Social, or Economic). Within those categories, the team will discuss each aspect alphabetically. For example, in the Economic category, the team will first discuss Aid, then Energy, and finally

Figure 1: Definitions

Definitions	
Diplomatic Ties	Political relations between North Korea and a specified country
Provocations	Unfavorable actions taken by North Korea aggravating a specified country
Aid	Money and provisions sent to North Korea from a specified country
Energy	Percent of energy resources exported to North Korea from a specified country
Trade	Transfer of goods for compensations between North Korea and a specified country
Illicit Activity	Illegal exchanges between North Korea and persons acting as private individuals within a specified country
Refugees	Individuals who flee from North Korea to a specified country
Remittances	Transfer of monetary or material support to North Korea from private individuals in a specified country

Trade. The team defines each of these aspects in **Figure 1**.

In addition, the team sought to determine potential leverage points from the perspective of each of the specified countries and to quantify these relationships. The key shown in Figure 2 was used to signify the strength of relationships between North Korea and a given country, ranging from a green circle which indicates a strongly positive relationship to a red circle indicates a strongly negative relationship. The circles with the "X" illustrate no current relationship. The blank circles indicate an unknown relationship as data was not available or was not significant enough to be determined.

Figure 2: Key

Key	
Strongly Positive Relationship	○
Slightly Positive Relationship	●
No Relationship	(X)
Slightly Negative Relationship	○
Strongly Negative Relationship	●
Unknown Relationship	○

In order to classify the strength of the relationship, the team first determined if the relationship was positive or negative. Then the quantity of goods, money, incidences, negotiations, or persons was compared across countries. This was used to decipher the quality of the relationship as "slight" or "strong", allowing the team to characterize relationships as strongly positive, slightly positive, no relationship, slightly negative, strongly negative, or unknown relationship.

Throughout this paper, the team will address the specified countries' perspective toward North Korea. The specified countries include China, Japan, Russia, and South Korea. For example, Provocations between North and South Korea refers to incidences where North Korea provoked the South, not vice versa. This is the team's understanding based on extensive research. After quantifying the relationships between North Korea and each of the specified countries, the team evaluated the United States's ability to leverage those points for each of the specified countries. The team's research focused on **current** bilateral relationships between North Korea and the specified countries.

In the Bilateral Relationships portion of the project, the team provides a step-by-step analysis of how these points were developed. Subsequently, the team compiled all of the bilateral relationship figures to create one summary figure. Finally, the team used the bilateral leverage points to determine potential US leverage points.

Please note, the bilateral relationships between North Korea and the specified countries are not rank ordered, but rather are analyzed in alphabetical order by the name of the specified country. Bilateral relationships are analyzed from the specified country's perspective, not from the perspective of North Korea.

STATE TO STATE RELATIONSHIPS

China – North Korea

Upon the conclusion of World War II, the Korean Peninsula was divided into northern and southern regions. Although the division was meant to be temporary, this resulted in the permanent establishment of the Republic of Korea, South Korea, and the Democratic People's Republic of Korea, North Korea, in 1948 (Nanto and Manyin, China-North Korea Relations). Alliances with both South Korea and North Korea began to form at the onset of the Korean War in 1950. The US, along with the United Nations, immediately defended South Korea. China, on the other hand, intervened with forces on behalf of North Korea. China suffered significant losses in population over the course of the Korean War. One estimate claims China's "combat losses were more than 360,000 (including 130,000 wounded) and noncombat losses were more than 380,000" (Aiping 137). By July 1961, eight years after the Korean War, China and North Korea formed a military alliance aptly named the Treaty of Friendship, Cooperation, and Mutual Assistance. The treaty required both countries defend the other upon attack (Nanto and Manyin, China-North Korea Relations 5).

Further strengthening the relationship, China reconstructed North Korea following the Korean War. China's motivation for reconstruction and investment in North Korea stemmed from multiple political considerations. First, Chinese leaders viewed North Korea as a critical buffer state between the Chinese border and American military forces stationed in South Korea (Nanto and Manyin, China-North Korea Relations 5). Second, reconstruction promoted an economically stable border state and minimized the influx of North Korean refugees across the PRC-North Korea border. As time passed, reconstruction benefitted both China and North Korea, their political relationship remained amicable until the early 1980's (Nanto and Manyin, China-North Korea Relations 6). The relationship changed when the People's Republic of China (PRC) initiated economic reforms that invigorated their markets. North Korea, conversely, was opposed to such reforms because they undermined regime control. Further complicating the relationship, China established full diplomatic ties with South Korea in 1992 (Nanto and Manyin, China-North Korea Relations). Despite speed bumps, the relationship between China and North Korea remains "the most enduring, uninterrupted bilateral friendship for both countries" (Scobell 1).

Figure 3 shows the bilateral relations between, by category, China and North Korea. As explained in the methodology section, a green circle indicates a strongly positive relationship. A red circle indicates a strongly negative relationship. A yellow circle indicates a slightly negative relationship. The blank circles indicate an unknown relationship as data was not available or was not significant enough to be measured.

Figure 3: China – North Korea Relationships

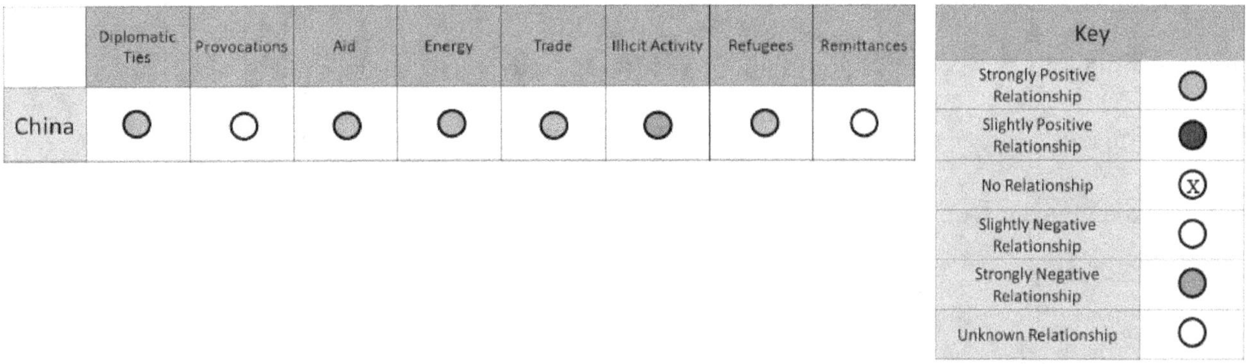

Political

North Korea's primary political ally is China. The China-North Korea political relationship was forged through shared socialist ideologies (Nanto and Manyin, China-North Korea Relations 5). Andrew Scobell, an Associate Research Professor at the Strategic Studies Institute, asserts that China's alliance with North Korea goes outside the bounds of having a friendly neighbor. Rather, the Chinese see North Korea as a way to legitimate the Leninist ideology (Scobell 2). China and North Korea are two of the few communist nations to survive collapse. Scobell argues that if Leninist regimes continue to collapse, it will be more difficult for China to justify the Chinese Communist Party's continued right to rule (Scobell 2). Foreign leaders have suggested the current Chinese leadership's primary focus for the decade ahead is the sustained power of the Chinese Communist Party (Scobell 2). As such, China can relate to the efforts North Korean leaders take to garner support.

Despite sharing ideologies, the quality of the China-North Korea political relationship has fluctuated. North Korea's nuclear pursuits, in spite of Chinese discouragement, have dampened the relations of senior leaders from both countries. Yet, China has stood by as their primary political ally.

The team believes China may be overlooking North Korea's nuclear pursuits to some degree in order to maintain its political strategy. China's political strategy is to promote stability on the Korean Peninsula in order to limit the number of North Korean refugees crossing its border. From China's perspective, supporting the Kim regime has been the best option in deterring an influx of refugees crossing the North Korean-Chinese border (Bajora 1). As such, China is backing Kim Jong-un during his succession as the next leader of North Korea. Because China's political goals remain unchanged, Kim Jong-un's recent succession is unlikely to significantly affect the political relationship with North Korea.

Diplomatic Ties

The central focus to accumulating diplomatic support within China and North Korea's borders is unification. Standing in the way of reaching that goal is called the frustration of "divided nation ideologies" (Scobell 2). North Korea is divided from its southern counterpart while China is divided from Taiwan (Nanto and Manyin, China-North Korea Relations 6). This frustration of "divided nation ideologies" perpetuates the political actions taken by Chinese and North Korean leaders. For example, leaders of China and North Korea have yet to take the use of force off the table to achieve unification (Scobell 2). The Chinese and North Korean defiance against their respective divided nations has resulted in a political standoff with the US backed South Korea and Taiwan.

Given the proximity of China and North Korea to their "divided nations", it should come as no surprise that certain locational considerations have shaped their political relationship. Because Japan used the Korean Peninsula in its attack of mainland China in the 20th Century, Chinese leaders understand the strategic importance of its 850 mile North Korean border (Scobell 3). Chinese vulnerability via the North Korean border quickly became apparent during the US intervention in the Korean War. According to Daniel Sneider of Stanford's Asia-Pacific

Research Center, "stability and the avoidance of war are the top priorities" for China (Bajora 3). In that sense, North Korea creates a huge problem for China because its provocations may unilaterally prompt a war. Not surprisingly, avoiding war is a key Chinese policy consideration in its relationship with North Korea.

Beyond threats of war, China's diplomatic ties with North Korea are largely impacted by North Korean refugees. Adam Segal, a Senior Fellow at the Council on Foreign Relations contends "the Chinese are most concerned about the collapse of North Korea leading to chaos on the border" (Bajora 3). In efforts to tighten its borders, China's government has made agreements with North Korea to deport their refugees (Nanto and Manyin, China-North Korea Relations 5). Additionally, the Chinese government has periodically allowed North Korean authorities to capture their refugees within China's borders. The North Korean refugees that are repatriated may be subject to "labor correction" or even execution (Nanto and Manyin, China-North Korea Relations 5).

Chinese political considerations—specifically securing the border it shares with North Korea—is prioritized despite outside political pressure. Chinese dealings with refugees have withstood significant pressure by the United Nations. Although China is a party to the United Nations refugee conventions, China justifies its actions by referring to North Korean refugees as economic migrants (Nanto and Manyin, China-North Korea Relations 5). The refugee convention states "no contracting State shall expel or return ("refouler") a refugee in any manner whatsoever to the frontiers of territories where his life or freedom would be threatened on account of his race, religion, nationality, membership of a particular social group or political opinion" (1951 United Nations Convention Relating to the Status of Refugees, Article 33). The Chinese government has not allowed United Nation agencies or non-governmental organizations to assist the ailing North Korea refugees (Nanto and Manyin, China-North Korea Relations 5). It appears the Chinese government is attempting to shield the rest of the world from the depth of the refugee problem on its border. China is known for limiting information flow regarding its government's questionable practices. For example, the oppressed Tibetan region is continually stripped of outside support due to Chinese intervention. Likewise, the Chinese government is shielding the world from aiding, and in some respects, understanding the gravity of the North Korean refugee situation (Nanto and Manyin, China-North Korea Relations).

The depth of the refugee problem in China will never fully be understood until further access is granted. Currently, information flow to the outside world regarding North Korean refugees is sparse and inconsistent. According to the State Department, there are between 30,000 – 50,000 North Koreans in China. However, non-governmental organizations estimate the number of refugees to be closer to 300,000 North Koreans in China (Margesson, Chanlett-Avery and Bruno 4). Until China allows the U.N. Refugee Agency or non-governmental organizations to have access to North Koreans, the rest of the world can only estimate the magnitude of the issue. It is, however, clear that China's political relationship and diplomatic ties with North Korea are largely affected by refugee concerns.

Provocations

Similar to refugee concerns, provocations have played a significant role in the Chinese-North Korea political relationship. Although China is North Korea's primary political ally, the relationship is not without nuance. Recent North Korean provocations perturbed Chinese leadership. Despite China's protests of North Korea's 2006 and 2009 nuclear tests, North Korea moved forward with the testing. China formally opposed the nuclear tests thereafter (Bennett). After North Korea's 2006 nuclear test, experts asserted that China began reconsidering the nature of its alliance with North Korea to now include both "pressure and inducements" (Bajora 1). Following North Korea's 2009 nuclear test, it became apparent that senior leaders of both countries maintained a tenuous relationship (Bennett). Council on Foreign Relations Representative Scott Snyder and See-won Byun of the Asia Foundation argue that the nuclear tests underline tensions between China's "emerging role as a global actor with increasing international responsibilities and prestige and a commitment to North Korea as an ally with whom China shares longstanding historical and ideological ties" (Bajora 1). This balancing act by China may be volatile as long as North Korea tests nuclear weapons against international pressures.

Although North Korea's nuclear testing is provocative by Chinese standards, many other North Korean acts, when compared to the mainstream international perspective are not. For example, China did not respond to North Korea's sinking of the South Korean warship Cheonan and the shelling of Yeonpyeong Island (Patience). Moreover, following North Korea's long-range missile test in 2006, China quietly sent an envoy to articulate their frustrations (Powell). On the other hand, following North Korea's 2006 nuclear weapons test, China publicly condemned North Korea by voting to impose UN sanctions against the North Korean government (Powell). As such, it appears Chinese leaders deem only nuclear tests as actual provocations. China has, after all, made clear for years that a nuclear North Korea is contrary to China's core interests (Powell). Although China's perception of North Korean provocations may be limited in scope, the Jane's information Group (2010) noted several issues it argues caused friction in the Chinese-North Korean relationship, including:

Figure 4 : Frictional Causes in Chinese – North Korean Relationship

- Chinese exasperation at the DPRK's failure to reform its economy;

- Pyongyang's prevarication over the nuclear and peace treaty issues and the consequent dangerous stimulus this provides to proliferation in the region;

- The nuclear standoff with the US and Pyongyang's possession of nuclear weapons; growing economic and political rapport between Pyongyang and Taipei;

- The North Korean refugee problem on the China-North Korean border; Pyongyang's missile testing, prompting Japan to acquire a Theater Missile Defense system, with Taiwan wishing to be included;

- North Korea's construction of underground missile site close to the Chinese border; and North Koreas cavalier attitude towards business[1] (Nanto and Chanlett-Avery, North Korea: Economic Leverage and Policy Analysis).

With some experts asserting that China has both "pressure and inducements" on the table in dealing with North Korea, China's actions to address its core interests may change in the coming years. If that is the case, then it is likely that the China-North Korea relationship may evolve moving forward to address North Korea's nuclear pursuits.

Economic

Although the China-North Korea political relationship continues to evolve in response to North Korea's nuclear program, it is hard to determine how their economic relationship may be affected. China's support for North Korea reaches well beyond politics to the realm of economic assistance. During the Cold War, North Korea relied on extensive support from the former USSR. Following the Soviet Union collapse, China's economic role in North Korea grew dramatically. Today, China is North Korea's largest aid, energy and trading partner.

Aid

China classifies its actual aid totals to North Korea as top secret **(Choo 349)**. One form of aid China provides North Korea is a trade discount, meaning the sale of goods at a below-retail rate. At $1.25 billion, China's trade discount alone exceeds aid provided by any other country **(Bajora 2)**. Beyond the trade discount, China also provides North Korea with food aid. China's fluctuating food aid totals to North Korea can be seen in Figure 5.

Energy

Like much of North Korea's economy, energy is provided both in the form of aid and trade. During the Cold War era, the former Soviet Union was North Korea's largest oil supplier. However, following the collapse of the Soviet Union, North Korea turned to China to fill the void (Choo 360). North Korea attempted to offset its oil dependence from counties like Iran, Libya, Syria, and Yemen, and ultimately relied predominantly on China (Choo 360).

Since 1997, North Korea has received energy related aid in the form of petroleum coke, diesel and oil from China. Through legitimate trade, North Korea primarily purchases oil due to minimal refinery capabilities.

Trade

The trade relationship is strongly positive, a result of $3.1 billion of total trade in 2011. North Korea's largest import and export partner is China. For example, 50% of North Korean exports go to China while 41% of North Korean imports come from China. In fact, trade rose 87% from 2010 to 2011 totaling $3.1 billion. Nonetheless, trade relations remain vulnerable to the influence of political developments. For example, trade rose substantially upon the collapse of the Soviet Union following the Cold War. Likewise, North Korea is now trying to increase trade relations with Russia in order to decrease its trade and dependence on China (People's Daily Online).

Figure 6 shows Chinese – North Korean trade figures between 1982 to 2009. As you can see, trade between the two countries has increased across time[1].

North Korea's strategically important economic sectors are food and energy. Food and energy are noteworthy because both sectors are supplemented and/or provided from China. For example, 30-40% of North Korea's total food is provided from China. Ninety percent of North Korea's non-aid food is supplied from China. Likewise, 70% of North Korea's energy resources are from China. In fact, China supplies North Korea with as much as 88% of its oil. The types of energy resources supplied from China include crude oil and coking coal. Coking coal differs from the raw coal that North Korea exports because it has been reprocessed. Much of North Korea's oil is used for manufacturing fertilizer in support of its agricultural industry as opposed to merely powering vehicles. In 2007, expert, Andrei Lankov, estimated there were only 20,000 – 25,000 passenger cars in all of North Korea, suggesting approximately one person per every one thousand had access to a private vehicle (Martin).

China invests in mineral rich and sea-port accessible areas. In February 2012, China agreed to invest $3 billion in North Korea's northeastern free trade zone. China is using this investment to create an export base. China will build an airport, power plant, cross-border railway and piers in

---

[1] UN Comtrade, Ministry of Commerce of the People's Republic of China as shown in *Integration in the Absence of Institutions: China-North Korea Cross-Border Exchange* by Stephan Haggard, Jennifer Lee, and Marcus Noland, August 2011.

the North's Rason economic zone bordering China and Russia by 2020. For its investment, China will have access to the port for 50 years. The Rason port will give China's northeastern provinces direct access to the Sea of Japan (Agence France - Presse (AFP)).

By limiting its investment to special economic zones, China is theoretically creating two North Koreas. One North Korea is developing and experiencing an influx of investment. Meanwhile, a second North Korea is still impoverished with little assistance from China. In essence, China's investment is widening the gap within North Korea between the "have's" and "have-not's" (S. Kim).

China, more than others, receives approval from North Korean authorities to invest. As such, China maintains a significant advantage over the competition—most notably, South Korea. China's investment is twofold. First, China seeks economic gains from minerals and port accessibility. Second, China's investment seeks to induce North Korea to initiate economic reforms. That being said, economic reforms in North Korea remain unlikely as it undermines regime control.

Similar to investment, China maintains an advantage for conducting cross-border trade with North Korea. Much of this trade arose during the famine in the 1990s. At that time, North Korea's public distribution system essentially failed, leaving millions starving. Households, work units, local party organs, government offices, and military units began entrepreneurial activities, albeit technically illegal in North Korea, to survive (Haggard and Noland, Reform from Below: Behavioral and Institutional Change in North Korea 2). Alas, the North Korean Black Market was born.

Information regarding the North Korean Black Market is murky, as the title may suggest. However, in 2008 The Peterson Institute surveyed 300 North Korean refugees living in South Korea to understand the development of the market (Haggard and Noland, Reform from Below: Behavioral and Institutional Change in North Korea). Though the following revelations are limited by a 300 person sample size, the survey is one of the few studies to analyze the state of North Korea's black market. The survey produced staggering statistics regarding the scope of marketization. Over 70% of those surveyed and 60% of their spouses engaged in private (illegal) trading activities in North Korea. Shockingly, nearly half of those surveyed report that *all* of their income was earned through private business.

Not surprisingly, residence in a town bordering China correlated with one's use of the black market as a source of income (Haggard and Noland, Reform from Below: Behavioral and Institutional Change in North Korea 8). In addition, experts from the Peterson Institute for International Economics conducted another case study on Chinese-North Korean cross-border exchange released in August 2011. The case study titled *Integration in the Absence of Institutions: China-North Korea Cross-Border Exchange* surveyed over 300 Chinese enterprises that are doing or have done business in North Korea. The study essentially painted a picture of what enterprises face when doing business in North Korea. As a caveat, not all Chinese enterprises surveyed engaged in business that is necessarily part of the black market. The results showed that there are principally two types of Chinese enterprises that engage in business with North Korea: large state-owned enterprises (SOE) and numerous smaller private businesses (Haggard, Lee and Noland, Integration in the Absence of Institutions: China-North Korea Cross-Border Exchange 3). When the Chinese enterprises were asked whether their North Korean counterparts were acting legally, they vaguely reported that SOEs were their main business partners (Haggard, Lee and Noland, Integration in the Absence of Institutions: China-North Korea Cross-Border Exchange 6). According to the Peterson Institute experts, North Korean SOEs come in three varieties. The first type of North Korean SOEs deal in legitimate, legally sanctioned business. The second type of SOE is those where the managers have exploited the company's legal status to surreptitiously engage in unrelated (and sometimes illicit activity). The third variety of a SOE in North Korea is those entrepreneurs affiliate with for political protection. For example, businesses may target an SOE to simulate a legitimate joint venture.

Regardless of who their North Korean counterparts are, the Chinese enterprises are often forced to engage in corrupt practices. One of the most common forms of corruption when doing business in North Korea is bribery. This is often used for contract enforcement, investment rights, cross-border travel, and security against expropriation. As mentioned above, the entrance of key players—notably local party structures, government offices, and military units—in the North Korean black market have perpetuated the bribery problem because they have the power to circumvent government intervention.

Fifty-five percent of businesses polled reported the need to bribe to do business (Haggard, Lee and Noland, Integration in the Absence of Institutions: China-North Korea Cross-Border Exchange 8). The survey suggests that investors must bribe more in comparison to traders. This may be due to investments requiring more contact with local officials, causing them to be at greater risk for expropriation (Haggard, Lee and Noland, Integration in the Absence of Institutions: China-North Korea Cross-Border Exchange 8).

Although key North Korean power-players are involved in cross-border trade, Chinese companies have been reluctant to trust their North Korean counterparts. As a result, less than 5 percent of the Chinese enterprises polled report extending a line of credit to North Koreans (Haggard, Lee and Noland, Integration in the Absence of Institutions: China-North Korea Cross-Border Exchange 10). In fact, most transactions are strictly cash payments upon delivery (Haggard, Lee and Noland, Integration in the Absence of Institutions: China-North Korea Cross-Border Exchange 15). By limiting business deals to cash, transactions are obviously limited in size when compared to a system with lines of credit.

Because Chinese enterprises are reluctant to extend credit, it would appear that North Korea's black market theoretically has a ceiling. However, it remains to be seen whether the black market has reached its plateau to this point. Regardless, it is fair to suggest that legitimate market reforms must take place before North Korean free trade reaches its potential.

Social

Immigration into China remains a huge concern. As mentioned before, the crux of China's policy toward North Korea hinges on limiting immigration. That being said, North Koreans do cross the border and return, both illegally and legally, for trade purposes[2]. In response to the famine during the mid-1990s, small-scale social units—households, work units, local party organs, government offices, and even military units—initiated entrepreneurial behavior to secure food (Noland 2009). To assure performance on this trading activity, bribery flourished as a contract enforcement method. As a result, a bribery relationship has arisen between China and North Korea. North Korea is trying to suppress these relationships but has been overwhelmingly unsuccessful. In fact, since Kim Jong-il's death, it costs North Korean traders five to ten times more money to bribe North Korean soldiers to cross into China (Los Angeles Times).

To enhance the bribery relationship, traders in North Korea use smuggled Chinese cell phones linked to Chinese towers. The latest figures from 2011 show that 809,000 North Koreans have cell phones on the Egyptian network. However, while the number of smuggled Chinese cell phones linked to Chinese towers is unknown. Considering the growing number of communication and bribery relationships occurring between China and North Korea, it is apparent that North Koreans are gaining considerable access to outside information.

---

[2] See above for discussion on black market trade and the perpetuation of the bribery relationship between China and North Korea.

Notwithstanding the illegal social ties China shares with North Korea, China is the largest source of the majority of tourists in North Korea. This legitimate social relationship is welcomed by the North Koreans to gain much needed money.

Illicit Activity

To be clear, North Korea's government sanctions illicit activity to gain much needed revenue. The Chinese "Triads", a prominent criminal syndicate, cooperates with North Korea to distribute and sell much of North Korea's illicit drugs. Additionally, North Korea's primary front company for illicit activities recently relocated from Macao to mainland China.

Refugees

The refugee relationship is strongly positive. The Chinese government agrees to return refugees to North Korea, and according to the State Department, there are between 30,000 – 50,000 North Koreans in China. However, non-governmental organizations estimate the number of refugees to be closer to 300,000 North Koreans in China.

Remittances

Like refugee information, the actual remittance totals sent from China to North Korea is unclear.

Japan-North Korea Relationship

Japan's primary interest with North Korea is nuclear stability. Japan's Ministry of Foreign Affairs released the statement, "The Government of Japan will aim to normalize the relationship with North Korea in a manner that would contribute to the peace and stability of the Northeast Asian region, in close co-ordination with the United States of America and the Republic of Korea" (Ministry of Foreign Affairs of Japan 1).

In many ways, "North Korea's hostile and suspicious attitude toward the outside world is a continuation of Korea's long tradition of isolation, seclusion, and defensiveness against external threats" (Armstrong). These negative feelings date back to the beginning of the Japanese occupation of the Korean Peninsula. Japan invaded Korea during the Russo-Japanese war of 1904-1905 and forced the emperor to sign a treaty permitting the Japanese to use the country as a military base and to place advisers in the Korean government. After the war, Japan set up a protectorate in Korea. In 1907 the king was forced to abdicate the throne in favor of his son. Three years later, Japan officially annexed Korea in 1910 (Encyclopædia Britannica). "Japanese colonialism was another authoritarian layer of experience, on top of Korean tradition, that has influenced present-day North Korea" (Armstrong).

At first, Japanese rulers claimed they wanted to preserve the Korean identity. The Japanese initially provided Korea with a more systematic and less corrupt government, and standards of public services, public health, education, and modern industry, also greatly improved. However, this soon changed, and after several years, Japan proved to be highly suppressive, self-centered, brutal, and unsympathetic (The World Today 190).

Although the Korean people were considered to be subjects of the Japanese emperor, they were not treated as equal to Japanese citizens. The Koreans were not able to publish their own newspapers or to organize into political or intellectual groups. Toward the end of the occupation, all Koreans were required to speak Japanese and were strongly encouraged to adopt Japanese names.

Korea was also stunted economically under Japanese rule. Almost all industries were owned by Japanese corporations. For example, in 1942 only 1.5 percent of total capital invested on the Korean peninsula was in Korean industries. Korean manufacturers were also charged with 25 percent higher interest rates than Japanese manufacturers placing Korea at a clear disadvantage (Library of Congress Country Studies 1,2,3).

Japan's treatment of the Korean people drastically worsened during the Second Sino-Japanese War and World War II. Japan forced Korean citizens into its military. In addition, from 1939 to 1945, Japan used approximately 5,400,000 Korean forced laborers to support its war operations coercing thousands of Koreans to move to Japan in order to make up for the labor shortage caused by the war. Work included forced labor on military bases, railroad construction sites, as well as in mines and plants across Japan (The People's Korea).

During World War II, Japan coined the term "comfort women." Experts estimate roughly 200,000 Korean comfort women were forced to work in Japanese military brothels (Hancocks). In her testimonial at a protest advocating for the compensation of comfort women in Seoul, Kim Bok-dong stated, "When I started, the Japanese military would often beat me because I wasn't submissive. Every Sunday, soldiers came to the brothel from 8am until 5pm, on Saturday from noon until 5pm, plus weekdays. It was very hard to handle. I couldn't stand at the end of the weekend. Since I had to deal with too many soldiers, I was physically broken" (Hancocks).

Many Koreans still resent Japan's harsh treatment during the occupation, and these negative feelings still affect Korean-Japanese politics today. It is difficult to determine exactly how many Koreans suffered or died as a result of Japanese mistreatment during the occupation; Korea was not invited to participate in the War Crimes Trial. North Korea still holds feelings of hostilities towards Japan for the treatment of the Korean people during the occupation and claim that Japan is partially responsible for the segregation of the Korean peninsula.

In addition, North Korea's nuclear threats further heighten hostilities. Before the discovery of

Figure 7: Japan – North Korea Relationships

	Diplomatic Ties	Provocations	Aid	Energy	Trade	Illicit Activity	Refugees	Remittances
Japan	◯	●	Ⓧ	◯	Ⓧ	◉	◯	●

Key	
Strongly Positive Relationship	◯
Slightly Positive Relationship	●
No Relationship	Ⓧ
Slightly Negative Relationship	◯
Strongly Negative Relationship	◉
Unknown Relationship	◯

North Korea's nuclear weapons program in 2002, most of the strain between Japan and North Korea was a result of social and humanitarian issues. However, Japan's concern especially shifted when North Korea withdrew from the Nuclear Non-Proliferation Treaty (NPT) in 2003 and Japan realized their country was at risk of a nuclear threat (BBC News). Overall, Japan has a strongly negative relationship with North Korea. Figure 6 shows the bilateral relations between Japan and North Korea.

Figure 6 shows the bilateral relations between Japan and North Korea. As explained in the methodology section, a red circle indicates a strongly negative relationship. A blue circle indicates a slightly positive relationship. The blank circles indicate an unknown relationship as data was not available or was not significant enough to be measured. The circles with an "X" indicate no relationship.

Political

Diplomatic Ties

Relations have been tenuous dating back to the Japanese Occupation of the Korean Peninsula. Japan does not have an embassy in North Korea; nor does North Korea have an embassy in Japan. Dealings remain argumentative due to the development of North Korea's nuclear program as well as other provocations. This represents the strongly negative diplomatic relationship between the two countries.

Provocations

The largest non-nuclear provocation was the abduction of the Japanese citizens in the 1970's and 80's. After Japanese citizens oddly started to disappear off of Japan's shores, Japan immediately began to suspect North Korea as having a hand in this activity. However, North Korea continuously denied all charges. Japan stated,

"The abduction is an important issue concerning the sovereignty of Japan and the lives and safety of Japanese citizens. Because North Korea has not provided an acceptable account with convincing evidence, the Government of Japan is demanding that North Korea take actions such as immediately returning the victims and providing a full account of those victims whose safety is unknown, based on the premise that all victims whose safety is unknown are still alive" (Ministry of Foreign Affairs of Japan).

Eventually, North Korea agreed to a summit meeting with Japan to discuss the issue. At the summit on September 17, 2002, North Korea officially admitted to and apologized for abducting Japanese citizens during the 1970s and 1980s. They also promised not to repeat similar behavior in the future (Headquarters for the Abduction Issue).

At the first summit meeting with Japan, North Korea stated there were only 13 abduction victims, four were alive, eight were dead, and 1 was unaccounted for. However, Japan was skeptical of this claim and demanded more details. North Korea offered the remains of one of the abductees, but the forensic analysis proved that the remains belonged to another individual (Headquarters for the Abduction Issue). Japan then demanded the investigation be reopened with the Japanese government active in the North Korean investigation.

Currently, the Japanese government asserts that 17 Japanese citizens were abducted by North Korea. The reasons given for the abductions were that the Japanese citizens were used as teachers in North Korean Spy training facilities. Their reasons for abduction were to teach North Koreans how to speak and act Japanese. As of October 15, 2002, North Korea released five of the abducted citizens to be reunited with their families in Japan. A few of the Japanese citizens had started families in North Korea during their abduction. The Japanese government strongly urged North Korea to ensure the family members' safety and to schedule a date for them to return to Japan as well. The safety and whereabouts of the remaining 12 victims is still to be determined but continue to be a serious subject for negation between Japan and North Korea (Headquarters for the Abduction Issue).

An additional provocation is North Korea's unwillingness to abandon their nuclear weapons program. Japan was a large advocate for the Six-Party Talks with North Korea. However, after North Korea's nuclear testing in 2006 and 2009, Japan began to feel increasingly threatened with the threat of nuclear instability; especially after North Korea withdrew from the Six-Party Talks. Japan is especially nervous with North Korea's upcoming satellite launch because many believe it is a disguise for a third long-range rocket launch. Thus, provocations between the two countries have caused a strongly negative relationship.

Economic

In the past, Japan maintained relatively strong economic relations with North Korea. Currently Japan has no trade relationships with North Korea primarily due to North Korea's refusal to abandon their nuclear weapons program.

Aid

From the mid-1990's to 2003, Japan sent 766,000 metric tons of food aid to North Korea to help lessen the effects of their food crisis (Manyin, Japan-North Korea Relations: Selected Issues 14). However, in 2004 when North Korea released the remains of another individual in the place of a Japanese abducted citizen, Japan only sent half of the promised 250,000 tons of food aid to North

Korea and does not plan to send more in the near future (BBC News). Prior to this incident, Japan was known for temporarily withholding aid to North Korea following certain provocations, but always resumed aid relief after a period of time. However, Japan is currently not providing North Korea with any aid. Thus the aid relationship with North Korea is unknown.

Energy

Japan has never been a large energy supplier to North Korea. Japan's main commodity exports to North Korea are luxury goods and machinery (Manyin, Japan-North Korea Relations: Selected Issues). In the past, North Korea supplied Japan with a large percentage of coal. However, all exchange relations were severed after the 2006 and 2009 nuclear testing. Thus Japan's energy relationship with North Korea is unknown.

Trade

For an extended period of time in the past, Japan had been one of North Korea's largest trade partners. When Soviet troops withdrew from Korea in 1948, Japan became North Korea's second-largest trading partner, holding 18 percent of all trade. North Korea's leading export items to Japan were men's suits, mushrooms, and coal. Japan's main export items to North Korea were cars, electrical components, woolen fabrics, and general machinery (Manyin, Japan-North Korea Relations: Selected Issues 12). After North Korea's missile tests in 2006, Japan took many measures to sanction trade between the two countries. These sanctions have caused Japan to put a ban on all imports and have restricted all North Korean ships from entering Japanese ports.

After the second nuclear and missile tests in 2009, Japan placed even tighter sanctions on North Korea and banned all exports to the country (BBC News). Thus, Japan does not currently engage in any trade relations with North Korea. Thus, the two countries share no trade relationship.

Social

Since the Japanese Occupation of Korea, there have been strong social ties between Japan and North Korea. However, these relations are not always seen as positive. There is a large population of native Korean residents living in Japan recognized as the Chosen Soren. The Chosen Soren is unified under the General Association of Korean Residents in Japan and is Korea's de facto embassy in Tokyo. Chosen was the formal name of Korea when it was a colony of Japan during the occupation. Japan does not have diplomatic relations with the North Korean nationals who do not change their nationality to South Korean. (General Association of Korean Residents in Japan) "Hundreds of thousands of ethnic Koreans were brought to Japan as forced laborers or migrants when the peninsula was a Japanese colony before 1945. Some have become Japanese citizens; others have South Korean passports, but a significant minority remain loyal to Pyongyang." (Buerk) The Chosen Soren have their own schools which are run by Chongryon, which is Korean for the General Association of Korean Residents in Japan. They also have their own newspapers and many wear the traditional Korean dress. Currently there are an estimated 700,000 ethnic Korean Residents living in Japan accounting for about 85 percent of Japan's resident alien population (Hays).

The Chosen Soren has a complex identity.

> "The families of most hail not from what is now North Korea, but from South Korea. Their grandparents left before the Korean War, which divided the peninsula. Their Loyalty to North Korea and Kim Jong-il is because they hope to see it unified again. 'It's not that we regard them as Dear Leader,' says Ri Song-chan, 'but we are taught in school, and it's something I believe to be important, to have pride in being Korean'" (Buerk).

The Chosen Soren does not share the same rights as Japanese citizens. For example, high school education in Japan is free for citizens in Japan. However, since the ethnic Korean residents do not share full citizenship, they are excluded from these subsidies (Buerk). Also, if a student attended a North Korean sponsored high school, they would not be accepted into a Japanese college since the North Korean sponsored high schools are not recognized by Japan. There are also laws in Japan that promote employment, marriage, and housing discrimination. These laws exist because in Japan's Nationality Act, "citizenship is based on 'blood' not birthplace" (Tsujiyama).

There is also animosity between the Japanese and ethnic Koreans on a social level.

> "Many Japanese regard the Koreans as rude, pushy, crude, inferior, and overly emotional. These perceptions were evident in Japanese folklore and artistry. In the old days there were several racist names for Koreans and songs with lyrics like 'Koreans sound like pigs.' Koreans think of the Japanese as deceitful, arrogant, untrustworthy and conceited. 'To be anti-Japanese is part of being Korean,' wrote Ian Buruma, author of *Wages of Guilt: Memories of War in Germany and Japan*. 'It goes with the territory so to speak. And nothing makes a Korean feel more Korean that to continue being angry about old Japanese atrocities. The fact that some Japanese continue to deny them offers them an incentive to keep the flame of resentment burning.'" (Hays)

The ethnic Koreans also bear great backlash when North Korea decides to fire a missile or conduct a nuclear test. After the missile testing in 2006, the Chosen Soren were harassed and assaulted by residents of Japan. There were protests outside the General Association of Korea Residents in Japan's Tokyo headquarters and many children were abused on their way to school

(On). These social interactions lead to a strongly negative social relationship between Japan and North Korea.

Illicit Activity

Additionally, Japan has a strongly negative relationship with North Korea regarding illicit activity. The Japanese Yakuza is a prominent criminal syndicate through which the North Korean government sponsors illicit activity. North Korea also uses the Chosen Soren to sponsor their illicit activity. Japan receives a large portion of counterfeit US dollars and illegal drugs from North Korea. The exact amount of illegal substances is unknown but some Japanese sources believe that half of the drugs imported into Japan originate from North Korea (Hurst 36). It was also discovered in 2003 that North Korea was receiving the majority of their missile parts from illicit trade with Japan. "In May 2003, a North Korean defector who once worked as a scientist in Pyongyang's missile program testified to a Senate Governmental Affairs Committee hearing that 'over 90 percent' of the parts for North Korea's missiles are smuggled aboard passenger ships by the Chosen Soren, the pro-North Korean Association inside Japan" (Manyin, Japan-North Korea Relations: Selected Issues 6). Once this was discovered, Japan charged with the ethnic Korean resident that allegedly tried to ship the material that was believed to be building weapons of mass destruction in North Korea. It was also discovered that the ethnic Korean resident was sending the shipments through Thailand which would then be sent to North Korea (Manyin, Japan-North Korea Relations: Selected Issues 6).

Since early 2003, the Japanese government has tightened their enforcement tactics on the export of potential dual-use items to North Korea. The Japanese coast guard began expanding safety inspections and safety searches for illegal contraband on North Korean cargo and passenger ships. "More than 70 percent of the 120 North Korean ships inspected in Japan from January to August 2003 were ordered to halt operations or received safety warnings, compared with a general average of 10 percent for all countries' shipping." (Manyin, Japan-North Korea Relations: Selected Issues 5) This significantly reduced bilateral trade between the two countries and creates a strongly negative relationship.

Refugees

There have only been three groups of North Korean refugees documented in Japan. The most recent instance of refugees was a group of three men, three women, and three boys who were found in a wooden boat off the coast of Japan on September 13, 2011. Preceding this occurrence, "A family of four arrived in 2007, 20 years after 11 crew members of a North Korean ship sailed into a Japanese port" (BBC News). Japan's typical protocol in dealing with North Korean refugees is to allow the refugees to recover at an immigration facility, and after being questioned by Japanese authorities they are sent to refugee facilities in South Korea where they can be better accommodated (BBC News). It is unknown whether or not undocumented refugees are living in Japan. Thus Japan's refugee relationship with North Korea is unknown.

Remittances

In 2010 Japan stated that remittances are to be capped at three million yen ($36,504 US dollars) per transaction. This is a decrease from the previous ten million yen ($121,680 US dollars). However, "Many analysts point out that those measures would have little affect on Pyongyang anyway, given that the low level of Japan-North Korea economic relations. Already stringent Japanese sanctions do not provide Japan much leverage in the first place" (Kang and Lee). Also decreasing the remittances to North Korea was Japan's economic crisis in the late 1980's to 90's because the personal wealth of the Chosen Soren decreased significantly and many of their credit unions filed for bankruptcy (Manyin, Japan-North Korea Relations: Selected Issues 14). After the Japanese government discovered the Chosen Soren were working through certain credit unions, many of the credit unions were forced out of commission because they were so heavily sanctioned by the Japanese government (Manyin, Japan-North Korea Relations: Selected Issues 14). Thus, there is only a slightly positive relationship between the two countries.

Russia-North Korea Relationship

The relationship between Russia and Korea has fluctuated between positive and negative for several decades. The bilateral relations between these two nations date back 120 years to the Korean Chosun Dynasty (Vorontsov 4). The length of the relationship has some underlying importance to the two nations, but as North Korea has demonstrated time and time again, this will certainly not be a major factor in influencing their behavior towards Russia. Beginning in the mid nineteenth century, Russia sought to expand its influence on the Korean peninsula. Since then, Russia's top priority with North Korea has been to foster the "preservation of peace and stability on the Korean peninsula" (Vorontsov 4).

The overall relationship between Russia and North Korea greatly improved when Joseph Stalin appointed Kim Il-sung to rule North Korea (Vorontsov 4). Kim Il-sung's appointment came after he received special administrative and military training with the Soviet army. The Russian – North Korean relationship further grew during Korea's struggle with the Japanese colonial

Figure 8: Russia – North Korea Relationships

	Diplomatic Ties	Provocations	Aid	Energy	Trade	Illicit Activity	Refugees	Remittances
Russia	●	○	●	●	◐	○	○	○

Key	
Strongly Positive Relationship	◐
Slightly Positive Relationship	●
No Relationship	
Slightly Negative Relationship	○
Strongly Negative Relationship	◐
Unknown Relationship	○

regime. In early "1910, the Russian Maritime Province, Primorye, became a base for Korean refugees and anti-Japanese guerilla fighters" (Vorontsov 4). By allowing Korea to use its land, Russia showed that it was willing to stand behind the Korean interests and help combat the Japanese. A little known fact is that the recently deceased Kim Jong-il or the "Dear Leader" was born in a Russian village called Viatskoe and was originally named "Yura" which is customarily a Russian name (Vorontsov 4).

Figure 8 shows the bilateral relations between Russia and North Korea. As explained in the methodology section, a green circle indicates a strongly positive relationship. A blue circle indicates a slightly positive relationship. A yellow circle indicates a slightly negative relationship. The blank circles indicate an unknown relationship as data was not available or was not significant enough to be measured.

Political

Diplomatic Ties

The 1990's were a pivotal time in the determination of direction for Russian and North Korean bilateral political relationships. During this time Russia developed a political relationship with North Korea while keeping two objectives in mind. The first of the two objectives was to "prevent the emergence of North Korea as a nuclear power and to preserve the Nuclear Non-Proliferation Treaty (NPT)" (Buszynski 109). The second objective was to "pursue [Russian] long term interests on the Korean Peninsula" (Buszynski 810). In Russia's mission to attain these objectives it realized that in order to be successful they must maintain a balanced relationship with North and South Korea. Thus, Russia's diplomatic relationship with North Korea is slightly positive.

This balancing act performed by Russia worked well until the Russian President at the time, Boris Yeltsin, visited Seoul in 1992. This trip was conducted as a possible way for Russia to gain diplomatic and treaty relations with both the North and South. However, South Korea took this opportunity to apply pressure on Russia to abandon the 1961 Treaty of Friendship with North

Korea. This treaty obligated Russia to automatically respond if the North was attacked (Buszynski 810-811). Even though the Treaty of Friendship between Russia and North Korea officially ended a year earlier, in 1991, both countries still adhered to its guidelines and protocols. Russia eventually ceded to South Korea's assertions, abandoning the Treaty of Friendship. The renouncement of this treaty divided Russia and North Korea for future relations. Russia asked "for an exchange of letters with the North to confirm the new understanding of the treaty, which Pyongyang refused" (Buszynski 812). Many viewed Yeltsin's renouncement of the 1961 treaty as a step away from Russia's goal to achieve a balance on the Korean Peninsula.

During this same time period, China established a stronger relationship with South Korea which distanced Russia from achieving their second political objective, to gain greater influence on the Korean Peninsula. China's growing presence in South Korea began to dominate Russia's influence. Thus, President Yeltsin addressed the National Assembly and declared that Russia would be suspending its military involvement with North Korea and would begin finalizing the details on an agreement with South Korea. After this decree "Russia's relations with North Korea were effectively frozen" (Vorontsov 5). Several reports have claimed that during this period "the new [Russian] liberal elite decided that maintaining ties with a 'totalitarian regime' did not meet Russia's democratic ideals" (Vorontsov 5). According to Foreign Minister Andrei Kozyrev in 1996, Russia stated that they had open trade routes involving the sale of weaponry to any nation or person who would like to do business except, of course, North Korea (Vorontsov 5). After many urgings by South Korea toward Russia to cut all ties with the North, Russia eventually agreed and "ended its bilateral ties and communications with the "Great Leader" of

North Korea, nearly destroying its formerly privileged position" (Vorontsov 6). This was partially in response to South Korea's guarantee of access to unlimited trade and investment opportunities, a guarantee that Russia never received.

As the relationship with North Korea looked dismal and irreparable, Russia began to realize that in order to achieve its original goals, they would have to rebuild their relationship with the North. Boris Yeltsin's term as president of Russia did little to increase the political bilateral relations between Russia and North Korea and instead did much to hinder the positive growth between these nations. After Vladimir Putin became president in 1999, Russia began to rekindle hope for a positive political future with North Korea. Knowing that Russia must have a strong relationship with North Korea, Putin's administration on signed a new treaty resembling the Treaty of Friendship. The Good Neighborliness, Cooperation, and Mutual Assistance Treaty was signed February 9, 2000 (Buszynski 814).

These agreements represented both Russia and North Korea taking obligations to abstain from partaking in any actions aimed to limit or violate another country's sovereignty (Vorontsov 12). After agreeing on these new premises, Vladimir Putin made a historical first ever trip to North Korea. The objective of this trip was to "overcome Russia's exclusion from the affairs of the peninsula". Consequently, Russia was one of the few to enjoy a relationship with North Korea where a dialogue could be held (Buszynski 814). President Putin significantly increased Russia's bilateral political relations with North Korea in a relatively short time after coming into power. A testament to Putin's effectiveness came from North Korean leader, Kim Jong-il who stated of

Vladimir Putin, "at last Russia had a leader with whom to do business" (Vorontsov 9). As it stands now, the leaders of Russia and North Korea have a relatively positive personal relationship as Putin has shown his support for the new North Korean leader, Kim Jong-un. Thus the overall diplomatic relationship between Russia and North Korea is slightly positive.

Provocations

The relationship between Russia and North Korea is stained. Historically, North Korea has challenged Russia's authority and trust through breaking contractual agreements and by exercising other adverse actions by government officials. Russia realized that punishing North Korea for unacceptable actions may do more harm than working around them. Some of these problems have come in more recent times, such as the incident in 2005 involving the Russian cargo ship, *Terney,* which was detained by North Korean officials for approximately 13 days. It is presumed that if it were not for intense negotiations between Russian and North Korean diplomats, the confinement period would have been much longer (Vorontsov 15). This only heightened tensions between leadership.

Other examples of provocations include North Korea's internationally disputed nuclear program and series of nuclear and missile tests. For example, North Korea's 2009 underground nuclear test caused many countries to encourage more economic sanctions on North Korea. Upon hearing of the possibility of increased sanctions, the Russian Foreign Ministry released a statement saying "if we approve a new Security Council resolution on this issue, we must refrain from approving new sanctions against the DPRK, because sanctions will bring an opposite effect" (People's Daily Online). Other provocations by North Korea involve the smuggling of illicit materials into North Korea from Russia, further inhibiting the relationship established between Russia and North Korea.

Vladimir Putin's efforts continue to benefit both Russia and North Korea. Throughout positive actions by both parties, "hopes for improved Russia-DPRK relations have become a reality. The trend of dynamic, high-level political exchanges between the two states continues to the present day" (Vorontsov 12). In addition both sides saw an unlimited expansion in political relations where about 40 intergovernmental and interdepartmental agreements were made (Vorontsov 13). However, Russia is ultimately concerned with stability along its border, and it is seeks to neutralize relations with both Korean states, balancing relationships with one side so that it does not harm relationships with the other (Vorontsov 8). Consequently, Russia appears to be limiting itself in the amount of influence it can achieve. For example, "Russia's ties with North Korea, along with Russia's influence (if any) on North Korean domestic or foreign policy, remaining very limited" (Blank 23). This is how Russia and North Korean political bilateral relations stand today and depending on how the recently re-elected President Putin and Kim Jong-un interact, there may be a positive increase or an unfavorable turn in political relations. Thus Russia's relationship with North Korea regarding provocations is unknown.

Economic

The economic relationship between Russia and North Korea is similar to their political relations, though, on a smaller scale. The economic relationship between these two nations has fluctuated between high involvement and investment from Russia in North Korean affairs to virtually no economic activity at all. Dr. David Kerr, Director of Durham University's Centre for Contemporary Chinese Studies and specialist on the foreign relations of the Russian Federation, furthered the generally accepted belief that Russia's interactions with North Korea are self-motivated, asserting, "Russia may be willing to sustain Pyongyang's search for economic and forms of support since this both increases Russia's independent role on the peninsula and postpones regime change until this can be achieved in an orderly fashion" (Kerr). With an ambitious Russia trying to increase its influential power on the peninsula it is not a surprise that Russia has been, for the most part, willing and responsive to North Korea's hints at developing business deals and opening underdeveloped trade routes.

Though North Korea preaches *Juche,* self-reliance, since its founding, North Korea has largely depended on other nations for its economic needs. The Soviet Union supplied many economic resources to North Korea after the destruction caused by the Korean War. Before China's intervention, "Soviet capital and technical assistance accounted for most of the foreign help in reestablishing an industrial sector. Throughout the Cold War, Moscow was the North's most important partner" (International Crisis Group 9). Yet, this relationship has since dwindled. As the Soviet Union supplied North Korea with nearly all economic resources needed after the Korean War, "Russia's commitment was a net loss: billions of rubles of DPRK debt are still outstanding [today]" (International Crisis Group 9). As a result, North Korea lost credibility in many financial markets around the world because they could not pay off the debt they owed to supporting nations.

Aid

North Korea's history has been marked with the country's desperate need of aid from outside

sources. As mentioned earlier, North Korea lacks self-sustaining technology and resources.

Except for the Kim family and elite of North Korea, many North Korean citizens are

malnourished and near starvation. In the latter part of 2011, North Korea was said to have "been

reeling under the effects of a food shortage brought on by a combination of bad weather and

years of economic negligence" (Schwirtz 2). Russia, being a political ally of the impoverished

state, has provided much food aid to those starving in North Korea. North Korea's weather and

varied geography, from lowlands to large mountains, does not provide for a steady growing

season, if one at all. Due to the unfavorable growing conditions, North Korea relies on foreign

aid to fill the gaps that exist in its domestic supply of food and resources. Adequate statistics

could not be found as to how much monetary aid Russia supplies North Korea. However, Russia

has given North Korea 50,000 tons of wheat in food aid (Schwirtz). It was common for Kim

Jong-il only to visit Russia unless there was a severe need for goods in North Korea or if a

significant governmental policy was being negotiated. In 2011, Kim Jong-il traveled to Russia

via an armored train; this trip was likely provoked by a critical need for aid. (Schwirtz 1). This

action by Kim Jong-il displayed to the world that North Korea understood the vitality of the

resources Russia could provide the starving nation.

As a result of Mr. Kim's trips to Russia and several high-level bilateral meetings, "Russia's

Foreign Ministry announced that Russia had made the first delivery of an expected 50,000 tons of food aid to North Korea" (Schwirtz 2). Many sources have labeled these 50,000 tons as primarily wheat. This was a tremendous step in Russia's plans to improve its influence on the Korean Peninsula. With Russia demonstrating its willingness to support North Korea's people, many believe that future arrangements between the two nations will be much more cordial and smoother in implementation than arrangements with nations who are seeking agreements with North Korea without first giving assistance. In a statement released in 2011 by Russia's Foreign Ministry, the Russian government viewed "this humanitarian operation as a contribution to the strengthening of our traditional neighborly relations between the peoples of our countries" (Schwirtz 2). Along with the 50,000 tons of food aid already sent, Russia agreed to the framework of the UN World Food Programme, which stipulated 6.2 thousand tons of flour, would be delivered to North Korea as humanitarian aid (Tass 1). Lastly in 2011, Russia, as part of their membership with the United Nations and the UN's World Food Program , sent food, valued at 5 million dollars to Pyongyang (Tass 1). Overall, Russia's aid relationship with North Korea is slightly positive.

Energy

Despite the overall growth in trade relations between Russia and North Korea, oil exports to North Korea began decreasing in 2006. Oil exports dropped 91.1% compared to the same period of the previous year (Petrov, Russia-DPRK Economic Relations 1). The 2006 decrease in oil trade does not affect the overall importance of trade between North Korea and Russia as "the oil and gas revenues that for several years guaranteed macroeconomic stability now appear insufficient" (Aleksashenko 31). Russia's economy is experiencing a decrease in population due to the ageing population and drop in the labor force. The country will soon need to look in other markets in order to make a profit.

Another project currently in the developmental stages is the trans-Siberian pipeline which Russia is hoping to span through North Korea in order to service South Korea. South Korean President, Lee Myung-bak and Russian Prime Minister Dmitry Medvedev voiced a desire to link the Russia and South Korea via a gas pipeline (Petrov, Russia-DPRK Economic Relations 1). If the proposal for the pipeline passes, this may be the most important upcoming economic event involving both of these nations. The projected gas pipeline, if routed through North Korea, could be a source of about $100 to $500 million a year for North Korea (Word Press 5). However, Russia and South Korea are concerned about relying on North Korean. Upon threats, provocations, or wanting international attention North Korea could block the flow of gas through the pipeline. If passed, this project is tentatively scheduled to begin construction in 2013 and will supply gas to South Korea in 2017 (Petrov, Russia-DPRK Economic Relations 1). Overall, Russia's energy relationship with North Korea is slightly positive.

Trade

 Several factors such as chronic energy and food shortages and policies resulting in extraordinary misallocation of human and material resources hinder North Korean economic growth (International Crisis Group 9). Many believe that North Korea's biggest hindrance is its totalitarian government; experts argue that if the borders were open, free trade could occur and the conditions within the country would improve.

Until the late 1980's, the Soviet Union helped North Korea develop its manufacturing sector. "The North's factories built with Soviet aid produced all its aluminum, more than 60 per cent of its electric power, 50 per cent of coal and petroleum and petrochemical products" (International Crisis Group 9) The Soviet Union also invested large amounts of human capital into North Korea, allowing over 2,000 technicians and workers as well as over 20,000 students to study and train within the Soviet Union. Additionally, over 6,000 Soviet technicians helped sustain North Korean development (International Crisis Group 9).

Trade between Russia and North Korea, has fluctuated drastically over the years. In comparison to other countries, Russia's trade relations with North Korea are relatively weak. This is primarily due to "Russia's limited financial resources and its weak position in the North Korean economy" (Vorontsov 13). The same source also states that there could be some potential for a strong positive growth in the Russian and North Korean trade relationship by pointing to past year's figures. The Brookings Institute stated that "commodity turnover between the two states had dropped from US$1 billion during the peak of the Soviet-DPRK trade in the late 1980s, to US$80 million in 1999" (Vorontsov 13). This decrease came after a period of time when there was minimal trade between the countries because during the "1990s as Russia recognized South Korea, it announced that trade with North Korea was to be conducted in hard currencies, and opted out of its bilateral defense agreement" (Congressional Research Service 57). This restriction of economic activity followed a period of prosperity between the two nations. Russia has been credited with providing resources to North Korea in efforts to help establish and cultivate a much stronger military force as well as begin to develop a more substantial manufacturing district with North Korea. During the high times of the nation's bilateral economic relations in 1998 "about 60% of North Korea's trade was with the Soviet Union. Much of the trade was in raw materials and petroleum that Moscow provided to Pyongyang at concessional prices" (Congressional Research Service 57).

Since the 1990s, economic relations between the nations has seen improvement and in 2006 "Russia reportedly agreed to write off some 80% of the $8 billion debt owed it by the DPRK" (Congressional Research Service 58). The outstanding debt "remains a stumbling block in most negotiations on new aid and development programs. However, this debt can potentially make trilateral Russian-Korean relations closer and stronger". Trade during the 20 year period from 1990 and 2010 has followed an erratic pattern. After just 6 years trade between the two nations "reached $213 million in 2004, an 80 per cent increase from the previous year; exports to Russia more than doubled in 2004 and imports from Russia increased by 75 per cent" (International Crisis Group 10).

Along with this forgiveness of North Korean debt by the Russians, the economic relationship between the two saw another increase in 2008. This year, "North Korea ranked 107th among Russia's sources of imports and 92nd in terms of markets for Russian exports". Despite these statistics seeming to be insignificant, Russia moved passed "Japan and Germany to become

North Korea's third largest trading partner" (Congressional Research Service 57). The major Russian exports to the DPRK include petroleum products, timber, coal, fish, and marine products, as well as 70 percent of North Korea's debt to Russia originating from unpaid-for weapons" (S. S. Kim 29).

Russia has also received several requests from North Korea to receive goods in exchange for much needed revenues or for forgiveness of the remaining outstanding debt. However, Russian companies are said to have no interest in doing business with North Korea, given an example of Russian companies being "decisively uninterested in North Korean minerals" (Lankov, Russia-North Korea Trade 3). With all of this considered, in 2010 "the volume of trade between these two countries was merely US$110 million" (Lankov, Russia-North Korea Trade 2). Compared with other nations' trading volumes, this amount is relatively small. For instance China and North Korea enjoy a much higher trade volume which in 2010 "was around US$3.4 billion, some 30 times larger than [North Korean] trade with Russia" (Lankov, Russia-North Korea Trade 2).

Today, the economic trade relationship between the two countries seems to be prospering with projects being developed to further connect Russia with North Korea economically. One of the biggest plans currently in the works between these two nations is the constructions of a trans-Korean railway. There is benefit in increasing these economic ties for both nations. For North Korea, however, "Russia is critical to North Korean security, since Russia shares a border with the DPRK, and Russian cooperation would be necessary to enforce any security guarantee" (Congressional Research Service 57). Fortunately, Russia is hoping to be able to link the entire

Korean Peninsula by "upgrading its railway connections with the DPRK and has been participating in ambitious plans to build the trans-Korean railway" (Congressional Research Service 57). With all that has been discussed in this section of the paper, The Russian and North Korean economic trade relations do not appear to be stable in the long run and should be handled with extreme caution as big increases and decreases in activity have been attributable to the smallest of actions from one nation to the other. Overall, Russia shares strongly positive trade relations with North Korea.

Social

The social relationship between Russia and North Korea is very weak, existing primarily due to North Korean attempts at adopting some of Russia's successful cultural and scientific practices. The two countries also engage in exchanges of illicit activity. In addition, it is important to note that Russia has been trying to further its own influence on the Korean Peninsula. The social relationship between these two countries was relatively unexplored prior to the late 1900s. Since then, many experts have been looking much more seriously into the benefits or consequences of such a relationship.

Beginning in the mid 1990s, Russia began to realize that if they wanted to assert power on the peninsula they must rebuild any relationships that had been previously damaged by the Yeltsin Era or form any relationships that had not yet been fostered. With this in mind, in 1996 the Ministers of Foreign Affairs in both Russia and North Korea signed an agreement that addressed diplomatic exchange as well as cultural and scientific cooperation between 1997 – 1998.

(Vorontsov 7). After signing this agreement, future cooperation was expected between the two countries.

However, shortly after this plan was signed, many incidences, both positive and negative, were documented. The strength of the social relationship between Russia and North Korea can be shown by the cultural cooperation as well as educational opportunities available to students who wish to study in either Russia or North Korea. Kim Jong-il made several trips to Russia, aimed at acquiring much needed resources for his country. Some also involved enriching the performing arts and cultural identity of North Korea. In 2001, Kim Jong-il visited Russia to see the theater program and other similar performing arts facilities. After visiting one ballet performance, "Kim Jong-il was deeply impressed by the Mariinsky Theater Ballet in St. Petersburg and decided to develop a ballet program in the DPRK" (Vorontsov 10). Shortly after Mr. Kim's visit to Russia, North Korean officials sent a letter requesting that Russia admit five North Korean students to the Mariinsky Theater's Vaganova Ballet Academy (Vorontsov 10). As a result, Russia granted two openings for North Korean students to study at the Vaganova Ballet Academy. Later in 2004, a new cooperation agreement was signed between the DPRK Academy of Sciences and the Russian Academy of Sciences (Vorontsov 15). Under this new agreement, there were two performances that visited Pyongyang that year; both of which were attended by Kim Jong-il (Vorontsov 15).

Performing arts have not been the only niche of Russia's society that North Korea has tried to adopt. North Korea has also shown great interest in several Russia schools and universities. In the 2000 - 2001 academic year, 10 state scholarships were awarded to North Korean students by the Russian Ministry of Education. One year later, scholarships allocated for North Korean students increased by 25. (Vorontsov 15). The following year, 32 additional students were given scholarships to study in Russia. One of the bigger obstacles that had to be overcome before any students were allowed to study in Russia was the fact that many professors and administrative officials had an inherent opposition to sending people out into the world and letting them experience how everyone else lives. Once this barrier was lowered many more students were allowed to study outside of North Korean borders (Vorontsov 15).

As the social relationship between Russia and North Korea strengthened, North Korea began accepting and adopting more Russian cultural affairs. On top of the Russian language being the most widely studied foreign language in North Korea, many high qualified Russian musical groups visit North Korea of which almost all were attended by Kim Jong-il. Unsurprisingly, with the social relationship at its peak, nearly 12,000 North Korean tourists visited Russia in 2004 (Vorontsov 14). Rarely had there been reports of tourists, especially in such great quantities, being allowed to venture outside of North Korea. Another unprecedented advance for Russian and North Korean relations was the 2006 revitalization of the Orthodox Church in North Korea, signifying a positive shift for Russia and North Korea (Vorontsov 11).

Illicit Activity

There have been many documented instances of criminal activities within the Russian Organized Crime (ROC). They have been known for conducting business with various other criminal groups. The ROC works with other major international organized crime groups, of which, many are Korean criminal groups (Center for Strategic & International Studies 2). The illicit activity between these two countries is very active and has been growing, especially in North Korea as conditions become more dire for its citizens. During 1997 some of the major illicit activities carried out between Russia and North Korea included international narcotics trafficking, money laundering, and counterfeiting (Center for Strategic & International Studies 2). This shows that North Korea and Russia have been and are still involved in illicit activities which can negatively impact economies and societies. Further, in 1999 officials in Russia stated that North Korea bought equipment made in Russia with foreign money acquired through drug smuggling into Russia (Defense and Foreign Affairs Strategic Policy).

North Korea smuggles drugs and enlists the use of counterfeit currency to gain supplies and resources. The Russian Far East is a hot spot for contraband and illegal equipment to be smuggled into North Korea. Intelligence officials in North Korea have enlisted the help of the Russian Mafiya to legally and illegally transfer weapons and military supplies from the Russian Far East to Central Asia. Second-hand weapons are inexpensive and easy to obtain. Even the DPRK's deflated currency and drug resources can still purchase fairly large numbers of weapons and ammunition (Defense and Foreign Affairs Strategic Policy). In this respect, the Russian Mafiya is highly regarded by the North Korean government and close enough bonds must exist for transactions, such as the one listed above, to occur. Dire living conditions in North Korea are forcing its citizens to go to extremes to acquire the basic necessities for survival. On many occasions it has been reported that North Korea engages in Japanese, Russian, and Chinese drug trafficking as a state enterprise for severely needed money (International Crime Threat Assessment). Lastly, in 2007 some experts asserted that drug sales were deminishing; Other leads seemed to indicate new distribution strategies were implemented in China, Japan, Russia, and South Korea" (International Crisis Group 13).

Refugees

Another important aspect regarding the social relationship between these two countries is the number of refugees from North Korea living in Russia. Historically, the refugees have not been greeted with a warm welcome from China and many other countries. Russia has been, for the most part, welcoming of North Korean refugees it receives and has not threatened them with sending them back, which would assuredly cause problems for the refugees and their families back in North Korea. As one source states, "Russia does not forcibly repatriate defectors in the same way as China, so they are able to marry and work there. The Russian police have been treating defectors as humanitarian refugees since 2005, aware that forcibly repatriated defectors risk public execution and that their families face punishment, too" (Petrov, Russia-DPRK Economic Relations 9). One way that many North Koreans escape into Russia is through the labor agreement between the two nations. North Korean workers are sent to Russian logging sites or mining locations and work in unbearable conditions and receive hardly compensation for their work. Many of these workers flee their worksite and escape into the tundra of the Russian Far East. In 2006 experts estimated approximately 600 defectors were living in Russia (Petrov, Russia-DPRK Economic Relations 9). Compared to China, which is one of North Korea's main allies, this number is an indication of Russia's understanding of the harsh conditions that North Korean's are faced with every day. Overall, Russia's relationship with North Korea regarding refugees is unknown due to the unidentified number of refugees living in Russia.

The current state of the social relationship between Russia and North Korea is very similar to what it has been in the past. Russian performing arts are still active in North Korea demonstrating the ability of these two countries to continue a relationship that was built decades before. The educational agreement between the two countries is still strong today where "North Korean students can be found in Russian schools" (S. S. Kim 31). Moving into the future there is a strong chance that "North Korean professionals could begin travelling again to Russia to gain experience and scientific know-how" (International Crisis Group 14). The social relationship between Russia and North Korea, holding everything else constant, appears to be growing in strength and could potentially be an area where the United States could leverage North Korean actions if the social interweaving continues between Russia and North Korea. Overall, Russia shares a slightly negative relationship with North Korea.

South Korea-North Korea Relationship

South Korea's primary interests with North Korea are promotion of stability, familial bonds, and historical ties. Prior to the end of World War II, the Korean Peninsula existed as one unified state under the control of the Japanese. When the Japanese lost the war in 1945, the Korean Peninsula was confiscated by the allies; Russia and the United States agreed to separate the peninsula along the 38th parallel with Russia in control of the North and the United States controlling the South.

5

Russia created a Stalinist Regime in the North, placing young revolutionary Kim Il-sung in power, and the United States created a democracy in the South with Syngman Rhee as President. On June 25, 1950, after years of political consternation Kim Il-sung's North Korean Peoples' Army invaded the South (Hickey). At first, the North advanced swiftly, easily forcing the South Korean troops to defend a line south of Seoul. By April 1951 with the help of UN forces, the South Koreans had counter-advanced, defending the 38th parallel (Hickey). Not long after, North and South Korea commenced to discuss an armistice. On July 27, 1953, two years after negotiations began, an agreement was officially signed, establishing a new border and creating a demilitarized zone (The History Channel).

Figure 9 shows the bilateral relations between Japan and North Korea. As explained in the methodology section, a green circle indicates a strongly positive relationship. A red circle indicates a strongly negative relationship. A blue circle indicates a slightly positive relationship, and the blank circles indicate an unknown relationship as data was not available or was not significant enough to be measured.

Figure 9: South Korea – North Korea Relationships

	Diplomatic Ties	Provocations	Aid	Energy	Trade	Illicit Activity	Refugees	Remittances
South Korea	◍	◍	●	●	●	○	◍	◍

Key	
Strongly Positive Relationship	○
Slightly Positive Relationship	●
No Relationship	
Slightly Negative Relationship	○
Strongly Negative Relationship	◍
Unknown Relationship	○

Political

Diplomatic Ties

While the Armistice was signed in 1953, this marks only a temporary ceasefire, not a formal end to the Korean War (Glionna). The two countries have engaged in many violent incidents despite the signing of the Armistice over 58 years ago. Political relations continue to reflect this violence. South Korea suspended tourism to North Korea as a result of the incident in July 2008 when a South Korean tourist was shot near Mount Kumgang (U.S. Department of State). Furthermore, South Korea does not have an embassy in North Korea; nor does North Korea have an embassy in South Korea.

In 2007, North and South Korea met for a three-day summit in Pyongyang and signed an agreement that encouraged the development of a Korean War treaty. The summit ended after North Korea agreed to dismantle its nuclear programs by the end of 2007. However, North Korea did not honor their word to disassemble their nuclear program; this further cemented distrust between the two countries (Amos and Kuhn).

On January 11, 2010 North Korea proposed a formal treaty to end the Korean War. The communist state asserted that such a treaty, combined with a lift on sanctions, would bring them back to the six-party talks (Glionna). However, many South Koreans were apprehensive; "We cannot say it is all good news", said one official from the South Korean Foreign Ministry (Glionna). As is evident, North Korea's nuclear threats have further strained their relationship. Thus, their diplomatic relationship is strongly negative.

Provocations

South Korea has complained of North Korean provocations in physical attacks, nuclear and missile testing, and cyber-attacks. There have been nine major violent incidents between the two countries since 1980. Figure 10 identifies each of these incidents. Recent exchanges include the sinking of South Korea's Cheonan Warship, killing 46 on March 26, 2010, the firing along the border in October 2010, and North Korea's shelling of Yeonpyeong Island in November 2010 which killed four people (Taiwan News).

Figure 10: North Korean – South Korean Provocations

Date	Incident
October 9, 1983	Landmark blown up in Burma, killing 4 South Korean Cabinet ministers and 16 others
November 29, 1987	Bomb planted on South Korean airliner, killing 115
September 1996	Submarine lands commandos on South Korean Coast; 1 captured; 1 unaccounted for; 24 shot dead by their own
June 15, 1999	Naval battle breaks out on Yellow Sea; 20 North Korean sailors sunk
June 29, 2002	South Korean ship sank, killing 6 in the Yellow Sea; 13 North Korean deaths
November 10, 2009	North Korean – South Korean navies exchange fire; North Korean patrol boat retreats in flames
March 26, 2010	Cheonan sunk by North Korean Torpedo
October 29, 2010	North Korea – South Korea exchange fire across their border
November 23, 2010	North Korea fires artillery shells on South Korean Island

After the two deadly incidents of 2010, the South Korean defense minister anticipated the North would resume provocations in 2012, making the 100 year anniversary of founder, Kim Il-song's birth. (Taiwan News). The United States and South Korea asserted that any provocations by the North would not be tolerated, and 'counter-provocation' planning was underway (Taiwan News). Just months later, in April 2012, North Korea launched a missile, claiming that its purpose was to put a satellite in orbit. Nevertheless, the launch was unsuccessful. "'Initial indications are that the first stage of the missile fell into the sea 165 km west of Seoul, South Korea…The remaining stages were assessed to have failed and no debris fell on land. At no time were the missile or the resultant debris a threat.'" (Schwarz). While North Korea reiterated that the launch was for satellite purposes, the international community widely recognized the incident as an attempt to test a ballistic missile. The United States and its allies warned that if North Korea continues to pursue its nuclear ambitions, its isolation will only intensify and the needs of its people will only become greater (Schwarz).

In addition to violent incidents or nuclear tests, North Korea has been allegedly responsible for several cyber-attacks. South Korea blamed the North for a cyber-attack in May 2011 that paralyzed agricultural cooperative, Nongnyup's computer network. As a result, files were deleted inhibiting 'tens of thousands of customers' from using their bank issued credit cards for more than a week (Yonhap News Agency). In addition, important data was damaged or destroyed. North Korea stands by their assertion that they were not involved in the hacking, but the internet protocol address was identical to that North Korea had attempted to use in past attacks (Yonhap News Agency). This incident was particularly significant because it marked "the first publically reported case of computer sabotage by one nation against a financial institution in another country" (Harlan and Nakashima). In addition, it showed that even a poor but aggressive country could obtain the tools to disturb one of the most technically "savvy" nations in the world, and with few targets in North Korea, there was little that South Korea could do to retaliate (Harlan and Nakashima). This is significant because North Korea could potentially target other countries – China, Russia, Japan, and others – in the same or similar ways. Moreover, cyber-attacks are costly. As a result of this incident, South Korea plans to spend approximately $476 million on cyber security before 2015 (Harlan and Nakashima).

In addition, South Korea opposed North Korea's 2006 and 2009 nuclear tests as well as their missile tests in 1998, 2006, and 2009 (New York Times). Conduction of these tests was viewed as hostile. If additional provocations occur, the South Korean government may feel pressure to respond. Hence, these provocations result in a strongly negative relationship.

Economic

While South Korea's economy is growing, that of North Korea seems to be declining. Figure 11 shows the disparity between the North and the South's GDP per capita between 1950 and 2008.

As the economic disparity grows, assimilation between North and South Korea becomes more challenging. South Korea has very few economic investments in North Korea. In large part, this is due to the lack of trust between the two countries. North Korea is notorious for making deals and then failing to honor them (Oh and Hassig).

Despite the failure of the North Korean government to follow through on its promises, many South Koreans pity those in the North as victims of human rights violations and economic disaster (Park). Experts estimate that hundreds of thousands of North Korean people have died of starvation and malnutrition since the 1980s while public rations went primarily to the wealthy. However, what few aid and trade projects South Korea has in the North exist to diffuse suffering, violence, and unrest as well as to avoid massive immigration and currency fluctuations.

Aid

South Korea's aid relationship with North Korea is slightly positive. Aid has become a vital organ of the Kim regime. In the 1990s, North Korea suffered one of the most devastating famines of recent history, killing approximately one fifth of its total population. Starvation and malnutrition rates remain high in North Korea with some families spending approximately 80% of their income on food (Haggard and Noland, Aid to North Korea).

South Korea has stepped in to help. There are several things that potentially motivate South Korea's assistance efforts. First, South Korea has strong and obvious social ties to North Korea. For hundreds of years, Korea existed as one unified state. The Korean War separated families, and the older population in South Korea still remembers this well, and many South Koreans pity the North Koreans; some aid is humanitarian in nature. At the same time, South Korea fears instability in the North as a mass flood of refugees or increased tension on the Peninsula could place extra strain on the South Korean economy. Thus, they provide aid to promote stability. Third, South Korea has used aid as a propaganda tool both within the South as well as in the North. Despite mass suffering, the North Korean government has propagated that its citizens are among the most fortunate in the world, especially in comparison to their South Korean neighbor. "The North Korean media continue to project this image, but thanks to South Korean goods and humanitarian aid that began to reach the North in the 1990s, most North Koreans have come to realize that South Koreans are quite wealthy" (Oh and Hassig). Third, South Korea has used aid as a leverage point, hoping to drive North Korea to the negotiation table or better yet, to dissolve its nuclear weapons program completely.

South Korea has remained an aid donor over the last 20 or more years. However, the quantity of aid sent has dramatically fluctuated over the last few years. Figure 12 shows South Korean

Assistance to North Korea between 1998 - 2009. The amount of aid transferred from North Korea was particularly high between 1998 - 2008, the years predicated in the Sunshine Policy, a policy aimed at separating the economic and political affairs of the two states. However, even during that period, there was a dip in aid in 2006, likely as a result of North Korea's missile and nuclear tests respectively in July and October of that year. Aid dropped in 2008, likely as a result of the abandonment of the Sunshine Policy, which separated the political and economic relations of the two countries. Finally, there was another large dip in aid in 2009, likely as a result of North Korea's 2009 missile and nuclear tests (New York Times). Although not shown in Figure 12, South Korean aid to North Korea has been especially low in recent years, falling from approximately $35.7 million in 2010 to about $17.5 million in 2011 (Choson Ilbo).

Energy

South Korea does provide oil to North Korea, though exact estimates of how much are unknown. In the Foreign Assistance to North Korea Congressional Report, it was stated, up to 90% of the North's oil comes from China. This leaves less than 10% to come from South Korea and all other international state suppliers (Foreign Assistance to North Korea, Congressional Research Service 2009). It is known that energy resources are vital to the smooth operation of the Kim Regime, and as South Korea provides part of this energy, this indicates an important tie between North and South Korea. Thus, the energy relationship is slightly positive.

Trade

Total trade between North and South Korea amounted to only $1.5 million in 2011. This relationship is tiny in comparison to the billions that North Korea trades with China or the hundreds of billions that South Korea trades with China and Japan (Choe A7). However, this small amount of trade fosters a positive but struggling relationship between the North and South, and while trade has reached extraordinarily low levels in recent years, largely as a result of political tensions, this has not always been the case.

The Sunshine Policy, enacted in 1998 under then president Kim Dae-jung, separated the political and economic relationships between North and South Korea. It gets its name and principle idea from Aesop's fable, *The North Wind and the Sun* (BBC News). In this story the sun and the wind tried to remove a man's coat (BBC News). While the wind violently tried to tear the coat off of the man, the sun shone brightly, and the man willingly removed it (BBC News). Through their implementation of the Sunshine Policy, the South sought to emulate the sun's passive approach to temper North Korea's hostility and to manipulate the North into abandoning its nuclear program (BBC News). The South hoped to build repertoire by stressing that it wanted to coexist peacefully with the North, rather than to demand a change in leadership or forced reunification. It was also aimed at improving humanitarian conditions and uplifting the North Korean economy. "… [T]he South gave rice, fertilizer and more to its northern neighbor… to build confidence without setting conditions or demanding immediate reciprocity" (BBC News).

Separating the economic and political relations with the North, South Korea allowed private firms to invest in North Korea; it also permitted Southern companies and non-governmental organizations to move north. Many of these businesses moved to the Kaesong Industrial Zone, formally developed in 2005 (BBC News). "The complex is just north of the demilitarized zone (DMZ) between the two countries, and is a rare example of North-South co-operation" (BBC News).

In some economic regards, the Sunshine Policy was successful. North and South Korea enjoyed increased economic cooperation, trade, and travel, throughout the years of the Sunshine Policy. However, the main security goals surrounding its implementation failed as the North refused to abandon its nuclear program (Caryl 31). And, after 10 years of not actualizing its primary goals, the Sunshine Policy disappeared with the politics of a new South Korean president, Lee Myung-bak in 2008 (BBC News).

Despite the abandonment of the Sunshine Policy as well as the 2006 and 2009 nuclear tests and violent provocations in 2010, the Kaesong Industrial Complex has remained open. The Complex employed about 47,000 North Korean workers and about 500 South Korean workers in 2010. The complex has firms which manufacture clothing and textiles, kitchen utensils, auto parts, semiconductor parts, and toner cartridges (Manyin and Nanto, The Kaesong North-South Korean Industrial Complex). The Kaesong Industrial Complex serves as one of the few tangible changes that came from the Sunshine Policy (BBC News). Not only does the Complex promote trade of goods, but also a trade of labor, paradoxically strengthening the weak ties that exist between the two countries. The trade relationship is, therefore, slightly positive.

Social

There is resentment on multiple levels with which North Koreans view South Koreans and vice versa. North and South Korea diverge politically. While the North remains a Stalinist Regime, the South embodies democracy. The two States are still at war with one another and have very different political allies. While political and economic differences do, in part, shape South Korean perception of individuals in North Korea, there are several social relationships that clearly endure.

The Korean Peninsula has a long history of foreign occupation. However, despite foreign rule, North and South Koreans have been able to maintain their common language, and they have pride in what remains of their shared Korean culture and heritage. After years of domination, the North Koreans who pride themselves on their independence and *juche,* self-reliance, ideology feel betrayed. The North Korean government has propagated that South Korea is like a colony subjugated under the United States as a foreign power. North Koreans question after all these years, 'How could the South Koreans allow themselves to be controlled by the US?' (S. Kim).

North Koreans have criticized South Koreans of becoming too materialistic, and too easily swayed by foreign ideologies (Oh and Hassig). "North Koreans formerly believed that South Koreans were virtual slaves of the Americans, living life in abject poverty. In the 2002 survey, fully 80 percent of North Korean defectors said that when they lived in North Korea, they would have agreed to the statement 'South Korea is a colony of the United States'" (Oh and Hassig).

Illicit Activity

Very little information has been published regarding illicit activity by North Korea bridging into South Korea. One report suggested that Bureau 39 of the North Korean government has been involved in a "hacking ring that exploited online gaming sites to win points and exchange them for cash, making $6 million in two years" (Chestnet Greitens). Aside from this report, information regarding illicit activity is largely unavailable. Thus, an open circle is used to mark an unknown relationship as not enough information was available on this topic to determine the strength of the relationship.

Refugees

Motivated by humanitarian and economic deprivation in the North, over 21,000 refugees defected to South Korea since the Korean War (BBC News). Figure 13 shows the annual number of refugees from North Korea into South Korea extending from 1993 to 2010 (International Crisis Group).

As evident in this graph, the number of North Korean refugees entering South Korea has dramatically increased since the early 1990s. Today, more than 21,000 North Korean refugees are living in South Korea (BBC News). This increased presence of North Korean refugees is

both politically uplifting as well as economically demanding.

Dating back to the Korean War, defectors have in part been used for propaganda purposes. South Korea still employs this practice. North Korean defectors have been used as political tools to show the economic and political success, the desirability of South Korean life, in comparison to the North (International Crisis Group). In addition, the older generation of South Koreans participated in the Korean War or heard heart-wrenching stories about families being broken along the border or as a result of ideological differences. North Korea has demanded that refugees be forcibly returned, but South Korea has refused. While South Korea does not formally encourage North Korean defection, once South Korea, refugees are recognized them as full citizens, receive resettlement assistance, and the South Korean equivalent of welfare checks (Harden).

However, South Korea has begun to feel the economic strain that just 21,000 refugees has placed on their economy; the South worries of the extraordinary consequences if North Korea should collapse. Most of the North Korean refugees are physically and mentally unhealthy; they suffer from malnutrition and the trauma of abuse and neglect from their experiences both in North Korea as well as their vulnerable journey to the South. In addition, the majority is uneducated and lack skills and social networking cues, increasingly making it difficult for them to find work. Moreover, North Koreans in North Korea are plagued by a lack of freedom and lack of choice. Thus, when refugees arrive in the South and are confronted with choices, such as what to eat, where to go, and what mode of transportation to use, they quickly become overwhelmed. Finally, North Koreans refugees face stereotypes such as lazy, prone to crime, and alcohol dependent (International Crisis Group). The refugee relationship is also strongly negative.

Remittances

The Ministry of Unification in Seoul estimates that North Korean refugees in the South send approximately $10 million back to their families in North Korea; other reports estimate between $5-15 million is sent annually from South Korea to North Korea (Plaza). Most often North Korean persons receive remittances via hand delivery, and it is easiest to transfer money where cell phone use is available for coordination along the Chinese border. The networks that facilitate remittance transfers are often the same as those used to smuggle people and illegal goods and media into and out of North Korea (Lankov, Remittances from North Korean defectors).

 The cost of transferring remittances is steep. "The transaction fee currently fluctuates at 20-30 per cent of the total, so from the $1,000 sent by a refugee from Seoul, only $700-$800 will reach her relatives. Nonetheless, the system is quite reliable and incidents when the money does not reach its intended destination are rare" (Lankov, Remittances from North Korean defectors). North Korean families generally use remittance money to purchase essentials; if they have money left over they may spend it on small business investments. "Judging by anecdotal evidence, such money seems to be used for investments by North Korean recipients, most of whom run small businesses or workshops" (Lankov, Remittances from North Korean defectors). Other times, the remittances are used to reunite families (World Bank). The help of a professional defection broker, an individual that facilitates defection from North Korea, costs approximately 2-3 million won. Depending on the distance of the family from the border, the age, and the health of those defecting, the cost of a defection broker can be much higher

(Lankov, Remittances from North Korean defectors). While sending funds is illegal in both countries, neither country makes an effort to stop it. According to a survey conducted by the Database Centre for North Korean Human Rights, 49% of North Korean refugees in South Korea regularly send money back North (Lankov, Remittances from North Korean defectors). For the North, remittances promote economic stability. For the South, remittances show North Koreans that South Korea is prosperous, not the failing US colony propagated by Pyongyang. Thus, the remittance relationship is strongly positive. Overall, South Korea has a strongly negative relationship with North Korea due to diplomatic ties, provocations, and refugees.

LEVERAGE

Bilateral Summary

Figure 14 shows a summation of North Korea's bilateral relationship with each of the specified

Figure 14: Bilateral Relationship Summary

	Diplomatic Ties	Provocations	Aid	Energy	Trade	Illicit Activity	Refugees	Remittances
China	◐	○	◐	◐	◐	◐	◐	○
Japan	◐	◐	Ⓧ	○	Ⓧ	◐	○	●
Russia	●	○	●	●	◐	○	○	○
South Korea	◐	◐	●	●	●	○	◐	◐

countries. In summary, China has the strongest association with North Korea illustrated by their green circles indicating the strength in aid, diplomatic ties, energy, refugee, and trade relationships. Japan has the weakest association with North Korea due to their negative diplomatic ties, illicit activity, and provocations. Russia has a slightly strong relationship with North Korea due to their diplomatic ties and energy relationship. Finally, South Korea has a slightly weak relationship with North Korea as a result of diplomatic ties, provocations, and refugees.

Potential US Leverage Points

Figure 15 shows points where the US could potentially leverage North Korea through specified countries. The team determined these points based on expert opinion and extensive research. For

Figure 15: Potential U.S. Leverage Points

	Diplomatic Ties	Provocations	Aid	Energy	Trade	Illicit Activity	Refugees	Remittances
China	✓			✓		✓		
Japan	✓					✓		✓
Russia				✓	✓			
South Korea	✓		✓	✓	✓			

example China's aid and trade relationship with North Korea was not included because experts emphasized that China would not be influenced by any other countries on those issues.

The team has cited historical examples to support its evaluation of these points. In 2003, China shut down an oil pipeline to North Korea as a warning to Pyongyang for its nuclear pursuits. Within three days, North Korea agreed to participate in three-party talks in Beijing, abandoning its previous demand for bilateral discussions with the United States (Savage 31). This demonstrates the effectiveness of China's leverage on energy resources to North Korea.

North Korea is believed to supply Japan with half of its illicit drugs. To decrease the illegal activity, Japan closed six Credit Unions through which the criminal syndicates were funneling money (Manyin and Nanto, The Kaesong North-South Korean Industrial Complex). This indicates Japan's willingness to crack down and put pressure on North Korea's government sanctioned illicit activity. As a result, North Korea must find alternative markets for their illicit activity.

One historical example of a transfer of a leverage point is in the oil sector. Prior to the fall of the Soviet Union, the USSR was the primary supplier of oil to North Korea. After the collapse, Russia was no longer able to provide the country with a stable supply. North Korea turned to China as their primary provider of oil. As a result, North Korea became heavily dependent on China for its supply of oil. Noting this dependence, North Korea could be influenced by China (Petrov, Russia-DPRK Economic Relations).

South Korean aid fluctuates due to changes in their political relations with North Korea. As previously mentioned, in 2010 South Korea provided $26.4 million. Three violent incidences occurred between the two countries in March, October, and November of that year. The following year, South Korean aid dropped to $17.5 million (Choson Ilbo).

In a dire situation, the US could potentially leverage these points through the specified countries. Some experts have indicated the potential of a mass exodus of North Koreans if the collapse of the Kim regime occurred. Experts have suggested the possibility of further military provocations in this scenario to unify the citizenry. Upon the occurrence of further provocations, a dire situation would exist in North Korea.

In that case, China could cut off oil to manipulate North Korean behavior. Japan's government could pressure North Korea through freezing additional credit unions affiliated with illicit activity or criminal syndicates. In response to China's oil reduction, Russia could influence North Korea by increasing or decreasing the amount of oil they provide. Likewise, South Korea could increase or decrease its aid to North Korea. As evident from the historical examples previously referenced, leveraging North Korea in a dire situation could be successful.

The viability of the United States using the specified countries to leverage North Korea depends on the severity of the situation and the aligning of interests. For example, the US encouraged the specified countries to put pressure on North Korea's nuclear ambitions through the Six Party Talks. Success in this endeavor stemmed from the aligning of interests between the United States and the specified countries.

FURTHER RESEARCH

Throughout the research process, experts in relevant fields and research articles have helped the team ascertain areas for further research. There are many concerns regarding North Korean futures. Four main topic areas deserve more time before the results are published: The extent leadership change in other countries would affect North Korea's economy and trade, North Korea's possible response to sanctions and outside pressures of denuclearization, The extent of North Korea's relationship with Australia, Vietnam, and Myanmar, and How multilateral relationships will affect North Korean alternative futures

The team has discovered leadership changes in countries other than North Korea have great potential to affect North Korea's economy and trade. The exact effects on North Korea's economy and trade need to be researched further. Many times the team found that leadership changes in countries other than North Korea impacted bilateral economic relations between the two nations. Recently, changes in leadership of other countries have affected North Korea's economy due to the limited but still outward expansion of trade with outside countries. Possible strategies which merit further research for finding more extensive data on this topic include conducting a second round of outreach to experts who focus on economic activity in North Korea and surrounding countries. This more detailed round of questions will address the effects of outside countries on North Korea's economy and trade as well as how this can be exploited in order to achieve intended results.

North Korea has historically had strong reactions to sanctions and outside pressures of denuclearization. The actions of North Korea are highly monitored and any predictions would take a much more in depth look at what North Korea is wishing to leverage with each country by its actions. More research is needed to determine how further sanctions will affect North Korea's decision making process.

The extent of North Korea's relationship with Australia, Vietnam, and Myanmar should be further researched due to possible aid and trade influences over North Korea. A study can be conducted on each countries imports and exports, and comparing those points to North Korean imports and exports to determine possible trading opportunities. The focus of the team's research was to identify the relationship North Korea has between China, Japan, Russia, and South Korea and to sort through the most influential relationships to find an approach that would be applicable at USSTRATCOM and the mission given to the team. Additional leverage points could be added to this report depending on the results of this further research of Australia, Vietnam, and Myanmar.

Lastly, the team briefly researched how multilateral relationships affect North Korean alternative futures. However, further research is needed to better understand what drives North Korea's decisions based on these relationships. Despite the benefits to North Korea for fully cooperating with China, Japan, Russia, and South Korea as well as many other nations, North Korea has chosen to act in such a way to hinder the realization of the maximum benefits of these relationships. Further investigation will discover how to these multilateral relationships affect North Korean alternative futures.

SUMMARY

Holding true to its reputation as the "Hermit Kingdom", North Korea is one of the least understood countries in the world. The United States as well as many other nations across the globe has repeatedly attempted to calm North Korea's hostile actions through peaceful means and negotiations. North Korea lacks many vital resources needed for a country to remain in existence. Thus, this provides leverage opportunities for the United States to coordinate with countries who supply North Korea with such resources. Through these countries, the US could apply pressure to successfully leverage North Korea to conform to peaceful means of negotiations and to curtail North Korean provocations. The purpose of this paper is to use open source knowledge to identify these potential leverage points that can be utilized by United States to effectively influence North Korea.

ABOUT THE AUTHORS

Morgan Eichman: Morgan Eichman is a junior at Creighton University studying International Relations with an emphasis on Research Design and Analysis. She is a member of the Dean's Honor Roll and is a contributing member to the Creighton community. She is involved in Creighton's International Relations Club and is also the President of Creighton's Model United

Nations Team. She recently competed in the American Model United Nations conference in Chicago as well as the World Model United Nations conference in Singapore.

Kathleen McGlynn: Kathleen is an undergraduate senior at Creighton University. She is pursuing a degree in International Relations with an emphasis on Research Design and Analysis. Under the Bisenius Research Grant, Kathleen recently created a national database of anti-trafficking organizations, aimed at combatting national and international sex trafficking. She also wrote a cookbook for children with severe gastrointestinal and esophageal disorders. In addition, Kathleen is the Co-founder and Chairman of the Board for national non-profit, NETwork Against Malaria. The organization was cited in the United Nations Malaria Module.

Collin O'Neill: Collin was born and raised in Omaha where he is part of a family of four including his mom, dad, and older brother. He attended Creighton Preparatory High School. Collin now attends Creighton University, studying Accounting and Finance. He is a member of the Pi Kappa Alpha Fraternity where he is the Internal Vice President. He enjoys playing basketball and hanging out with friends.

Scott Thorson: After growing up in Nebraska, Scott and his wife ventured to Tulsa, Oklahoma for his first two years of law school. Upon recognizing that home would always be Omaha, the two recently moved back to Nebraska in order to finish up school at Creighton. When Scott is not in the classroom, it is likely he could be found at any one of the local golf courses. Scott's passion for golf can only be surpassed by his love for travel with his wife. Having met in New Zealand, the couple shares the indelible itch for travel and adventure.

BIBLIOGRAPHY

"1951 United Nations Convention Relating to the Status of Refugees, Article 33." n.d.

Agence France - Presse (AFP). "China 'agrees' to invest $3 bln in N.Korea trade zone." 2012. AFP. 13 May 2012 <http://www.google.com/hostednews/afp/article/ALeqM5gvZKnRbDWdUxviM1JgZzL2PLuYag?docId=CNG.3857041cbe5bc4267b095d487378e348.311>.

Aiping, Zhang. "China's People Liberation Army Vol. 1." 1994.

Aleksashenko, Sergey. "Russia's Economic Agenda to 2020." International Affairs (2012): 31-48.

Amos, Deborah and Anthony Kuhn. "North, South Korea Pledge to Seek Peace Treaty." 4 October 2007. NPR. 6 April 2012 <http://www.npr.org/templates/story/story.php?storyId=14980806>.

Armstrong, Charles K. Some Historical Perspective. 2012. 2 March 2012 <http://www.pbs.org/wgbh/pages/frontline/shows/kim/them/historical.html>.

Bajora, Jayshree. "The China-North Korea Relationship." 2010.

BBC News. "Japan bans exports to North Korea." 16 June 2009. BBC News. 1 December 2011 <http://news.bbc.co.uk/2/hi/8102602.stm>.

—. "Japan freezes food aid to N Korea." 14 December 2004. BBC News. 30 May 2012 <http://news.bbc.co.uk/2/hi/asia-pacific/4091833.stm>.

—. "Japan sends nine North Korean refugees to South Korea." 4 October 2011. BBC Asia News. 13 January 2012 <http://www.bbc.co.uk/news/world-asia-pacific-15163099>.

—. "Japan sends nine North Korean refugees to South Korea." 4 October 2011. BBC News. 6 April 2012 <http://www.bbc.co.uk/news/world-asia-pacific-15163099>.

—. "Sunset for Korean Sunshine Policy?" 28 March 2008. BBC News. 20 March 2012 <http://news.bbc.co.uk/2/hi/7317086.stm>.

—. "Sunset for Korean Sunshine Policy?" 28 March 2008. BBC News. 30 May 2012 <http://news.bbc.co.uk/2/hi/7317086.stm>.

—. "Timeline: North Korea." 17 December 2011. BBC News. 6 April 2012 <http://www.bbc.co.uk/news/world-asia-pacific-15278612>.

Bennett, Dr. Bruce. Research Leader: Strategy, Force Planning, and Counterproliferation Scott Thorson. 14 October 2011.

Blank, Stephen J. "Russia's Prospects in Asia." 2010.

Buerk, Roland. North Koreans in Japan remain loyal to Pyongyang, BBC News. 27 October 2010. 2011.

Buszynski, Leszek. "Russia and North Korea: Dilemmas and Interests." (2009).

Caryl, Christian. "The Hermit Kingdom." Foreign Policy (2009): 31-32.

Center for Strategic & International Studies. "Russian Organized Crime." Task Force Report. 1997.

Central Intelligence Agency. The World Fact Book. n.d. 3 April 2012 <https://www.cia.gov/library/publications/the-world-factbook/geos/kn.html>.

Chestnet Greitens, Sheena. "A North Korean Corleone." 3 March 2012. New York Times. 6 April 2012 <http://www.nytimes.com/2012/03/04/opinion/sunday/a-north-korean-corleone.html?_r=1&pagewanted=print>.

Choe, Sang-hun. "North Korea Warns South Over Military Drill but Accepts Food Aid." New York Times 28 January 2012: A7.

Choo, Jaewoo. "Mirroring North Korea's Growing Economic Dependence on China: Political Ramifications." University of California Press Journals (2008): 343-372.

Choson Ilbo. "DPRK Child Nourishment." 26 March 2012. North Korean Economy Watch. 27 March 2012 <http://www.nkeconwatch.com/category/health-care/epidemics/>.

Congressional Research Service. "North Korea: Economic Leverage and Policy Analysis." 2009.

Defense and Foreign Affairs Strategic Policy. 1999.

Encyclopædia Britannica. Kojong. 2012. <http://www.britannica.com/EBchecked/topic/321192/Kojong>.

General Association of Korean Residents in Japan. 2012. <globalsecurity.org>.

Glionna, John M. "North Korea seeks Korean War treaty, end to sanctions." 12 January 2010. Los Angeles Times. 6 April 2012 <http://articles.latimes.com/print/2010/jan/12/world/la-fg-north-korea-talks12-2010jan12>.

Haggard, Stephan and Marcus Noland. "Aid to North Korea." August 2007. Peterson Institute for International Economics. 4 April 2012 <http://www.iie.com/publications/opeds/oped.cfm?ResearchID=797>.

—. Reform from Below: Behavioral and Institutional Change in North Korea. Working Paper Series. Washington D.C.: Peterson Institute for International Economics, 2009.

Haggard, Stephan, Jennifer Lee and Marcus Noland. Integration in the Absence of Institutions: China-North Korea Cross-Border Exchange. Working Paper Series. Washington, D.C.: Peterson Institute for International Economics, 2011.

Hancocks, Paula. Time running out for Korean 'comfort women'. 7 March 2012. 13 3 2012 <http://www.cnn.com/2012/03/06/world/asia/korean-comfort-women/index.html>.

Harden, Blaine. "N. Korean Defectors Bewildered By the South." 12 April 2009. The Washington Post. 9 April 2012 <http://www.washingtonpost.com/wp-dyn/content/article/2009/04/11/AR2009041100766_pf.html>.

Harlan, Chico and Ellen Nakashima. "Suspected North Korean cyberattack on a bank raises fears for S. Korea, allies." 29 August 2011. The Washington Post with Foreign Policy World. 6 April 2012 <http://www.washingtonpost.com/world/national-security/suspected-north-korean-cyber-attack-on-a-bank-raises-fears-for-s-korea-allies/2011/08/07/gIQAvWwIoJ_story.html>.

Hays, Jeffrey. KOREANS IN JAPAN: DISCRIMINATION, CITIZENSHIP, NORTH KOREAN SCHOOLS AND JAPANESE WIVES IN NORTH KOREA. July 2011. 2012 <http://factsanddetails.com/japan.php?itemid=635&catid=18>.

Headquarters for the Abduction Issue. More on the Abduction Issue. Tokyo, Japan: Secretariat of the Headquarters for the Abduction Issue, 2011.

Hickey, Michael. "The Korean War: An Overview." 21 March 2011. BBC History. 6 April 2012 <http://www.bbc.co.uk/history/worldwars/coldwar/korea_hickey_01.shtml>.

Hurst, Cindy A. "North Korea: Government-Sponsored Drug Trafficking." Military Review September-October 2005: 36,37.

Hyung-Gon Jeong, Hokyung Bang. "An Analysis of North Korea's Principal Trade Relations." 2010.

International Crime Threat Assessment. "North Korea's Role in International Drug Trafficking." 1999. FAS.org. 29 2 2012 <http://www.fas.org/irp/threat/pub45270chap3.html#r6>.

International Crisis Group. North Korea-Russia Relations: A Strained Friendship. Update Briefing. Seoul/Brussels: International Crisis Group, 2007.

—. "Strangers at Home: North Koreans in the South." 2011.

Kang, David and Ji-Young Lee. "Japan-Korea Relations: Pyongyang's Belligerence Dominates." Comparative Connections (2009): 3.

Kerr, Dr. David. Interview. Scott Thorson. 2011.

Kim, Samuel S. "North Korean Foreign Relations in the Post-Cold Was World." Government, U.S. Strategic Studies Institute, 2007. 24-92.

Kim, Steven. Associate Professor, Asia-Pacific Center for Security Studies Kathleen McGlynn and Scott Thorson. 22 November 2011.

Lankov, Andrei. "Remittances from North Korean defectors." East Asia Forum 21 April 2011.

—. "Russia-North Korea Trade." East Asia Forum 6 October 2011: 2-5.

Library of Congress Country Studies. "Korea Under Japanese Rule." Country Study. 1990.

Los Angeles Times. "Kim Jong-il's death could prompt North Korean elite to flee." 24 December 2011. Los Angeles Times. 14 May 2012 <http://webcache.googleusercontent.com/search?q=cache:N1bmngZwp-kJ:latimesblogs.latimes.com/world_now/2011/12/north-korean-elite-may-flee-in-light-of-kim-jong-ils-death.html+five+to+ten+times+more+money+to+bribe+North+Korean+soldiers+to+cross+into+china&cd>.

Manyin, Mark E. and Dick K. Nanto. "The Kaesong North-South Korean Industrial Complex." Congressional Research Service Report for Congress. 2011.

Manyin, Mark E. "Japan-North Korea Relations: Selected Issues." CRS Report for Congress. 2003.

Margesson, Rhoda, Emma Chanlett-Avery and Andorra Bruno. "North Korean Refugees in China and Human Rights Issues: Internation Response and U.S. Policy Options." Congressional Research Service Report for Congress. 2007.

Martin, Bradley K. "In Kim's North Korea, Cars Are Scarce Symbols of Power, Wealth." 9 July 2007. Bloomberg. 14 May 2012 <http://www.bloomberg.com/apps/news?pid=newsarchive&sid=a31VJVRxcJ1Y>.

Ministry of Foreign Affairs of Japan. Japan-North Korea Relations. May 2004. 2012
    <http://www.mofa.go.jp/region/asia-paci/n_korea/relation.html>.

—. The Abductions of Japanese Citizens by North Korea. Tokyo: Ministry of Foreign Affairs of Japan,
    2011.

Nanto, Dick K. and Emma Chanlett-Avery. "North Korea: Economic Leverage and Policy Analysis."
    Congressional Research Service Report for Congress. 2010.

Nanto, Dick K. and Mark E. Manyin. "China-North Korea Relations." Congressional Research Service for
    Congress. 2010.

New York Times. "North Korea's Nuclear Program." 29 February 2012. The New York Times. 11 April
    2012
    <http://topics.nytimes.com/top/news/international/countriesandterritories/northkorea/nuclea
    r_program/index.html>.

"North Korea's Conflict with the South: timeline." 23 November 2010. The Telegraph. 10 January 2012
    <http://www.telegraph.co.uk/news/worldnews/asia/southkorea/8153048/North-Koreas-
    conflict-with-the-South-timeline.html>.

Oh, Kongdan and Ralph Hassig. The Hidden People of North Korea. Lanham, Maryland: Roman &
    Littlefield Publishers, Inc, 2009.

On, So Chung. So Chung On, General Association of Korean Residents in Japan. 9 November 2006. 2011
    <http://www.fccj.or.jp/node/1556>.

Park, S. John. Senior Program Officer (Northeast Asia), Center for Conflict Analysis and Prevention
    Kathleen McGlynn and Scott Thorson. 12 December 2011.

Patience, Martin. BBC News. 24 November 2010. 29 March 2012 <http://www.bbc.co.uk/news/world-
    asia-pacific-11828846>.

"People's Daily Online." 25 May 2009. People's Daily Online. 2 2012
    <http://english.people.com.cn/90001/90777/90853/6665383.html>.

People's Daily Online. "China's trade with N. Korea soars 87%." 24 October 2011. People's Daily Online.
    17 May 2012 <http://english.people.com.cn/90778/7624425.html>.

Petrov, Leonid. "Russia-DPRK Economic Relations." Asia Times 24 July 2008: 1-3.

—. "Russia-DPRK Economic Relations." Asia Times 24 July 2008: 1-3.

Plaza, Sonia. <u>People Move: a blog about migration, remittances, and development</u>. 28 July 2011. 2012 <http://blogs.worldbank.org/peoplemove/node/1379>.

Powell, Bill. <u>TIME Magazine</u>. 28 May 2009. 29 March 2012 <http://www.time.com/time/world/article/0,8599,1901416,00.html>.

Priest, Dana and William M. Arkin. "A Hidden World, Growing Beyond Control." <u>The Washington Post</u> 19 July 2010.

Savage, Timothy L. "China's Policy Toward North Korea." <u>International Journal on World Peace</u> (2003): 29-35.

Schwarz, Tim. "North Korea Rocket Breaks up in Flight." 17 April 2012. <u>CNN.</u> 7 May 2012 <http://www.cnn.com/2012/04/12/world/asia/north-korea-launch/index.html>.

Schwirtz, Michael. "With North Korea in Need, Kim Jong-il Goes to Russia." <u>The New York Times</u> 20 August 2011: 1-3.

Scobell, Dr. Andrew. "China and North Korea: From Comrades-in-arms to Allies at Arm's Length." 2004.

Taiwan News. "U.S., S Korea join hands against N Korea provocations." 29 October 2011. <u>Taiwan News Online.</u> 6 April 2012 <www.taiwannews.com/tw/ettn/print.php>.

Tass. "Russia sends flour to North Korea." <u>The Voice of Russia</u> 3 October 2011: 1.

The History Channel. "This Day in History: Armistice Ends the Korean War." n.d. <u>History.com.</u> 4 April 2012 <http://www.history.com/this-day-in-history/armistice-ends-the-korean-war>.

The People's Korea. <u>N., S. Korean & Japanese Urge Early</u> . 1998. <http://www1.korea-np.co.jp/pk/054th_issue/98080505.htm>.

The World Today. "Korea Past and Present." <u>Royal Institute of International Affairs</u> (1946): 182-184.

Tsujiyama, Yasunori Fukuoka and Yukiko. "Mintohren: Young Koreans Against Ethnic Discrimination in Japan." <u>The Bulletin of Chiba College of Health Science</u> n.d.

U.S. Department of State. "Korea, Democratic People's Republic of Country Specific Information." n.d. <u>Travel.State.Gov: A Service of the Bureau of Consular Affairs.</u> 9 April 2012 <http://travel.state.gov/about/about_4955.html>.

Vorontsov, Dr. Alexander. <u>Current Russia - North Korea Relations: Challenges and Achievements</u>. Washington, DC: The Brookings Institute, 2007.

Word Press. "Russia, North Korea Settle Pipeline Deal." 24 August 2011.

World Bank. 2011. 2012 <http://blogs.worldbank.org/peoplemove/node/1379>.

Yonhap News Agency. "S. Korea renews calls on North Korea to stop cyber attacks ." Yonhap News
    Agency 11 May 2011.

www.ingramcontent.com/pod-product-compliance
Lightning Source LLC
Chambersburg PA
CBHW081842280526